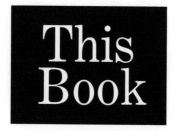

This
Book

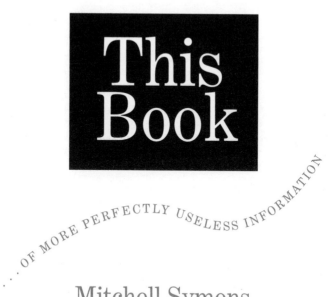

This Book

...OF MORE PERFECTLY USELESS INFORMATION

Mitchell Symons

HarperEntertainment

An Imprint of HarperCollins*Publishers*

HarperCollins books may be purchased for educational, business, or sales promotional use. For information please write: Special Markets Department, HarperCollins Publishers, 10 East 53rd Street, New York, NY 10022.

FIRST U.S. EDITION

Designed by Chris Welch

Printed on acid-free paper

Library of Congress Cataloging-in-Publication Data

Symons, Mitchell.
    This book— of more perfectly useless information / Mitchell Symons.—
1st ed.
        p. cm.
    Originally published: London : Transworld, 2004.
    Includes index.
    ISBN-13: 978-0-06-082823-3
    ISBN-10: 0-06-082823-4 (alk. paper)
    1. Handbooks, vade-mecums, etc. I. Title.

AG106.S94 2005
031.02—dc22   2005051108

---

05 06 07 08 09 ❖/RRD 10 9 8 7 6 5 4 3 2 1

A smattering of everything and
a knowledge of nothing.
—CHARLES DICKENS

It is possible to store the mind with a million facts
and still be entirely uneducated.
—ALEC BOURNE

If an idea's worth having once,
it's worth having twice.
—SIR TOM STOPPARD

This
Book

Pure Trivia, I

Trivia was a Roman goddess to whom sacrifices were offered at crossroads. Because travelers often engaged in idle gossip at crossroads, Trivia's name (referring to three roads coming together) came to be associated with the sort of information exchanged in such places.

Donald Duck's middle name is Fauntleroy. Quackmore Duck is the name of Donald Duck's father.

During U.S. conscription for World War II, there were nine documented cases of men with three testicles.

Eighty-two percent of the Beatles music was about love.

The name Wendy was made up for the play *Peter Pan*.

The pitches that Babe Ruth hit for his last-ever home run and that Joe DiMaggio hit for his first-ever home run were thrown by the same man.

Every time Beethoven sat down to write music, he poured ice water over his head.

Venetian blinds were invented in Japan.

Alfred Hitchcock didn't have a belly button. It was eliminated when he was sewn up after surgery.

Windmills turn counterclockwise.

The Nike swoosh was invented by Caroline Davidson back in 1971. She received $35 for making the swoosh.

The name of the character behind bars in the Monopoly board game is Jake the Jailbird.

Half the world's population has seen at least one James Bond movie.

Naturalists use marshmallows to lure alligators out of swamps.

Twenty percent of all road accidents in Sweden involve an elk.

The name Yucatán comes from the Maya for "listen to how they speak"—which is what the Maya said when they first heard the Spanish.

M&M's were developed so that soldiers could eat chocolate without getting their fingers sticky.

> **An ant lion** is neither an ant nor a lion. It is the larval form of the lacewing fly.

The bark of the redwood tree is fireproof. Fires in redwood forests take place inside the trees.

> **Amethyst** was once thought to prevent drunkenness.

Fifty percent of Americans live within 50 miles of their birth-place.

Firsts

The first time women and men used separate toilets was in 1739 at a Paris ball.

> **Ice cream cones** were first served at the 1904 World's Fair in St. Louis.

Dubbed laughter was used on American television for the **first** time on September 9, 1950.

> **The first toilet tank** seen on U.S. TV was on *Leave It to Beaver.*

Dr. W. S. Halstead was the **first** to use rubber gloves during surgery in 1890.

> **The first** sport to have a world championship was billiards, in 1873.

3

Benjamin Franklin was the first person to suggest daylight savings time.

The first in-flight movie was shown on a Lufthansa flight on April 6, 1925.

The first couple to be shown in bed together on U.S. prime-time TV was Fred and Wilma Flintstone.

Austria was the **first** country to use postcards.

John Lennon's first girlfriend was named Thelma Pickles.

The first product to have a bar code was Wrigley's gum.

The first plastic ever invented was celluloid in 1868. It's still used today to make billiard balls.

The first mosque in the United States was built in 1893.

Sugar was first added to chewing gum in 1869— by a dentist.

The first telegraph message tapped by its inventor, Samuel Morse, was "What hath God wrought?"

Iceland was the first country to legalize abortion, in 1935.

The first words spoken on the telephone by its inventor, Alexander Graham

Bell, were "Watson, come here, I need you."

Whoopi Goldberg acquired her first name because she had a problem with flatulence.

The first words spoken on the phonograph by its inventor, Thomas Edison, were "Mary had a little lamb."

Captain Cook was the first man to set foot on all continents (except Antarctica).

In 1776, Croatia was the first country to recognize the United States.

Beethoven's Fifth was the first symphony to include trombones.

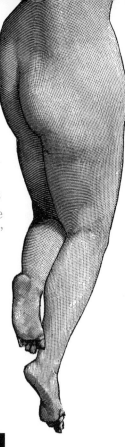

First Lines of Classic Novels

"It was a cold bright day in April, and the clocks were striking 13." (*1984* by George Orwell)

"Hale knew, before he had been in Brighton three hours, that they meant to murder him." (*Brighton Rock* by Graham Greene)

"As Gregor Samsa woke one morning from uneasy dreams he

found himself transformed in his bed into a gigantic insect." (*Metamorphosis* by Franz Kafka)

"**Last night I dreamed** I went to Manderley again."
(*Rebecca* by Daphne du Maurier)

"**Happy families are all alike,** but an unhappy family is unhappy in its own way." (*Anna Karenina* by Leo Tolstoy)

"**There were 117 psychoanalysts** on the Pan Am flight to Vienna and I'd been treated by at least six of them." (*Fear of Flying* by Erica Jong)

"**What's it going to be then, eh?**" (*A Clockwork Orange* by Anthony Burgess)

"**Many years later,** as he faced the firing squad, Colonel Aureliano Buendía was to remember that distant afternoon when his father took him to discover ice." (*One Hundred Years of Solitude* by Gabriel García Márquez)

"**Stately, plump Buck Mulligan** came from the stairhead, bearing a bowl of lather on which a mirror and a razor lay crossed." (*Ulysses* by James Joyce)

"**I'm going to get that bloody bastard** if I die in the attempt." (*King Rat* by James Clavell)

"On top of everything, the cancer wing was number 13." (*The Cancer Ward* by Aleksandr Solzhenitsyn)

"If you really want to hear about it, the first thing you'll probably want to know is where I was born, and what my lousy childhood was like and how my parents were occupied and all before they had me, and all that David Copperfield kind of crap, but I don't feel like going into it, if you want to know the truth." (*The Catcher in the Rye* by J. D. Salinger)

The First Records They Bought

Brian May: "Rock Island Line" (Lonnie Donegan)

Moby: "Live and Let Die" (Wings)

Mick Hucknall: "God Save the Queen" (The Sex Pistols)

Samantha Mumba: "Sisters Are Doin' It for Themselves" (The Eurythmics and Aretha Franklin)

Paul McCartney: "Be-Bop-A-Lula" (Gene Vincent)

Beginnings

Leonardo da Vinci invented an alarm clock that woke the sleeper by rubbing his feet.

Kiwis lay the largest eggs (relative to body size) of any bird.

Human babies born in May are on average 200 grams heavier than babies born in other months.

The word "sex" was coined in 1382.

From fertilization to birth, a baby's weight increases 5 billion times.

Clark Gable was listed on his birth certificate as a girl.

One female mouse can give birth to 100 babies in a year.

When Harold Robbins was a child, he used to run errands for Lucky Luciano.

A newborn kangaroo is small enough to fit in a teaspoon.

Bela Lugosi, the great screen Dracula, was actually born in Transylvania.

Numbering houses in London streets began only in 1764.

When a polar bear cub is born, it can't see or hear for the first month.

The first novel written on a typewriter was *The Adventures of Tom Sawyer.*

The ancient Greeks believed that boys developed in the right-hand side of the womb and girls in the left.

Paper was invented early in the second century by a Chinese eunuch.

Mel Gibson broke the school record for the most whippings in a week—27.

Pamela Anderson was Canada's Centennial Baby, having been the first baby born on the centennial anniversary of Canada's independence.

The drinking straw was invented in 1886.

Daryl Hannah was so shy as a child that at one point she was diagnosed as borderline autistic.

Carbonated soda water was invented in 1767 by Joseph Priestley, the discoverer of oxygen.

Screwdrivers were first used to help knights put on armor.

As a child, Sheryl Crow used to pretend she was Stevie Wonder by playing piano with the lights off.

The smoke detector was invented in 1969.

The wristwatch was invented in 1904 by Louis Cartier.

Emily Watson and Dido were banned from watching TV as children.

Sylvester Stallone was kicked out of 14 schools in 11 years.

Jodie Foster was mauled by a lion when she was a child.

Carnegie Hall in New York City opened in 1891 with Tchaikovsky as guest conductor.

Were Foster Children

Vidal Sassoon, Sylvester Stallone, Eartha Kitt, Marilyn Monroe, Barbara Stanwyck, Seal (until his Nigerian mother reclaimed him), Rosie Perez, Samantha Morton

Born with a Club Foot

Dudley Moore, Josef Goebbels, Mother Teresa, Emperor Claudius, Lord Byron, Callan Pinckney

Born in India

Spike Milligan, Joanna Lumley, William Makepeace Thackeray, Cliff Richard, Julie Christie, Engelbert Humperdinck, George Orwell, Lindsay Anderson, Vivien Leigh, Pete Best

Born in Canada

Saul Bellow, William Shatner, k. d. lang, Joni Mitchell, Bryan Adams, Rick Moranis, Leonard Cohen, Margot Kidder, Mary Pickford, Genevieve Bujold, Michael J. Fox, Donald Sutherland, Leslie Nielsen, Lou Jacobi, Mike Myers, Shania Twain, Jason Priestley, Michael Ondaatje, James Randi, Robbie Robertson, Natasha Henstridge, Alanis Morissette, Jim Carrey, Norman Jewison, Raymond Massey, Martin Short, Linda Thorson, Oscar Peterson, Christopher Plummer, Céline Dion, Norma Shearer, John Candy, David Cronenberg, Wayne Gretzky, Neil Young

Born in Wales

Heather Small, Christian Bale, Ryan Giggs, the Edge, Jonathan Pryce, Michael Owen, Shirley Bassey, Ioan Gruffudd, Catherine Zeta-Jones, Terry Jones, Timothy Dalton, Ray Milland, Roald Dahl, Me-One, Charlotte Church, Roger Rees

Born in Scotland

Sean Connery, Alan Cumming, Sheena Easton, Tony Blair, Robbie Coltrane, David McCallum, Annie Lennox, Maxwell Caulfield, Hannah Gordon, Lulu, Ewan McGregor, Midge Ure, Donovan, Sharleen Spiteri, Jimmy Somerville, John Hannah, Shirley Manson, Mark Knopfler, Ian Anderson, Billy Connolly, Jackie Stewart, Tom Conti, Jack Bruce, David Byrne, Marti Pellow, Irvine Welsh, Robert Carlyle, Jim Kerr

Born in Germany

John McEnroe, Andre Previn, Jackson Browne, Bruce Willis, Lucien Freud, Ruth Prawer Jhabvala, Henry Kissinger, Jeri Ryan, Martin Lawrence

Born Part Irish

Muhammad Ali, Joan Baez, Dolly Parton, Anthony Quinn, Emilio Estevez, Charlie Sheen, Robert Mitchum, Valerie Harper, Don Ameche, Lucille Ball, Marlon Brando, James Clavell, Alex Haley, Kiri Te Kanawa, Robert De Niro, Freddie Prinze Jr., Lindsay Lohan

Gypsy Blood

Elvis Presley, Eric Clapton, Django Reinhardt, Eric Cantona, Bob Hoskins, Charlie Chaplin, Ava Gardner, Pablo Picasso, Nadja Auermann, Miguel de Cervantes, Yul Brynner

Native American Blood

Burt Reynolds (one-quarter Cherokee)

Johnny Depp (part Cherokee)

Waylon Jennings (part Cherokee and part Comanche)

Cher (part Cherokee)

Mike McShane

Tiger Woods

Johnny Cash (one-quarter Cherokee)

Lena Horne (one-eighth Blackfoot)

Jimi Hendrix (part Cherokee)

James Garner (part Cherokee)

Roy Rogers (part Choctaw)

Kim Basinger (part Cherokee)

Dolly Parton (one-eighth Cherokee)

Dennis Weaver (part Osage)

Eartha Kitt (half Cherokee)

Farrah Fawcett (one-eighth Choctaw)

Sandy Duncan (part Cherokee)

Chuck Norris (half Cherokee)

John Phillips (half Cherokee)

Sally Field (part Cherokee)

Redd Foxx (one-quarter Seminole)

Joe Montana (part Sioux)

Johnny Ray (part Blackfoot)

Oral Roberts (part Cherokee)

Will Rogers (part Cherokee)

Tommy Tune (part Shawnee)

Tori Amos (part Cherokee)

Jerry Hall (part Cherokee—her mother's father's grandmother was a Cherokee)

Val Kilmer (part Cherokee)

Jessica Biel (part Choctaw)

Hilary Swank

Winston Churchill (one-sixteenth Iroquois)

Carmen Electra (part Cherokee)

Lou Diamond Phillips (one-eighth Cherokee)

Shannon Elizabeth (part Cherokee)

N.B.: Benjamin Bratt's mother, a Peruvian Indian, is an activist for Native Americans

The Human Condition

If your body's natural defenses failed, the bacteria in your gut would consume you within 48 hours, eating you from the inside out.

Only 4 percent of babies are born on their due date.

People who smoke have 10 times as many wrinkles as people who don't smoke.

15

Women smile more than men do.

People who suffer from gum disease are twice as likely to have a stroke or heart attack.

We use 43 muscles to frown.

We use 17 muscles to smile.

The fastest-moving muscle in the human body is the one that opens and closes the eyelid.

Fourteen million people were killed in World War I; 20 million died in the flu epidemic that followed it.

Right-handed people tend to scratch with their left hand, and vice versa.

It takes the typical person 7 minutes to fall asleep.

Every year there are more births in India than there are people in Australia.

Someone who eats little is said to eat like a bird—even though many birds eat twice their weight in a day.

Men have on average 10 percent more red blood cells than women.

One square inch of human skin contains 625 sweat glands.

The islets of Langerhans are a group of cells located in the pancreas.

Most people have lost 50 percent of their taste buds by the time they reach age 60.

Fifteen million blood cells are produced and destroyed in the human body every second.

The **surface area of a human lung** is equivalent to that of a tennis court.

The hydrochloric acid in the human stomach is strong enough to dissolve a metal nail.

The **largest cell** in the human body is the ovum; the smallest is the sperm.

There are over 100 million light-sensitive cells in the retina.

The opposite of **"cross-eyed"** is "wall-eyed."

We use 54 muscles every time we step forward.

The **human head** is a quarter of our total length at birth, but an eighth of our total length by the time we reach adulthood.

Between the ages of 20 and 70, the typical person spends about 600 hours having sex.

Our **hearing is less sharp** after eating too much.

The hardest bone in the human body is the jawbone.

The **foot** is the most common part of the body bitten by insects.

The most sensitive cluster of nerves is at the base of the spine.

By **lying on your back** and raising your legs slowly, you can't sink in quicksand.

The longest recorded tapeworm found in the human body was 33 meters in length.

Vegetarians live longer and have more stamina than meat eaters, but they have a higher chance of getting blood disorders.

An eyelash lives about 5 months.

There are approximately 100 million acts of sexual intercourse each day.

In an average lifetime, a person will walk the equivalent of 3 times around the world.

Men get hiccups more often than women do.

Every year 100 people choke to death on ballpoint pens.

The color red has been found to promote the hunger reflex in humans. This is why so many fast-food establishments use the color in their logos and décor.

A human eyeball weighs an ounce.

Only 30 percent of people can flare their nostrils.

The average adult has about 18 square feet of skin.

A human being loses around 40 to 100 strands of hair a day.

A person will die from total lack of sleep more quickly than from starvation. Death will occur after about 10 days without sleep; starvation takes a few weeks longer.

If you go blind in one eye, you lose about a fifth of your vision but all your sense of depth.

The human body contains enough iron to make a 3-inch nail.

Women have more genes than men, and because of this they are better protected from things like color-blindness and hemophilia.

It takes about 200,000 frowns to make a permanent wrinkle.

The average nipple size is 0.27 inches for women and 0.22 for men.

The risk of a heart attack is higher on a Monday than on any other day of the week.

Intelligent people have more zinc and copper in their hair.

At 90 degrees below zero, your breath will freeze in midair and fall to the ground.

One out of every 200 women is endowed with an extra nipple.

Women are twice as likely as men to have panic attacks.

Schizophrenics hardly ever yawn.

The best way for a man to know whether he will go bald is to look at his mother's father.

An average pair of feet sweats a pint of perspiration a day.

There are twice as many left-handed men as there are left-handed women.

It takes about 150 days for a fingernail to grow from cuticle to fingertip.

Women have a higher incidence of tooth decay than men.

Vision requires more brain power than do the other four senses.

Women can detect smell better than men can.

Men can read smaller print than women can.

Women can hear better.

The average beard grows 5 inches a year.

The average newborn baby cries 113 minutes a day.

In one day an average person will take about 18,000 steps.

Women's hair is about half the diameter of men's.

The cartilage in the nose never stops growing.

The average person opens the fridge 22 times a day.

The average clean-shaven man will spend five months of his life shaving and will remove 28 feet of hair.

If you live to age 70, your heart will have pumped 55 million gallons of blood.

In a lifetime you eat around 35 tons of food.

The average reader can read 275 words per minute.

The vocabulary of the average person consists of 5,000 to 6,000 words.

In the adult human body, there are 46 miles of nerves.

When you stub your toe, your brain registers pain in 1/50 of a second.

The size of your foot is approximately the size of your forearm.

You burn 3.5 calories each time you laugh.

Women blink twice as often as men.

The kidneys use more energy than the heart (kidneys use 12 percent of available oxygen; the heart uses 7 percent).

The most common disease in the world is tooth decay.

You inhale about 700,000 of your own skin flakes each day.

Eighty-three percent of people hit by lightning are men.

Human thighbones are as strong as concrete.

The thumbnail grows the slowest, the middle nail the fastest.

When you sneeze, your heart stops.

The average life span of a taste bud is 10 days.

According to medical experts, babies dream in the womb.

Men are 4 times more likely than women to sleep naked.

The average person's eyes will be closed about 30 minutes a day because of blinking.

You'd have to walk 34 miles to melt away one pound of fat.

The body's largest internal organ is the small intestine, with an average length of 20 feet. The large intestine is only a sixth of the length of the small intestine.

The right lung takes in more air than the left (because the left lung is smaller, to make room for the heart).

Women have a wider peripheral vision than men do.

The average person grows up to 6 feet of nose hair in a lifetime.

It takes 25 muscles to swallow.

More people are allergic to cow's milk than to any other food.

Nonsmokers dream more than smokers.

The mouth produces 2 pints of saliva a day.

Teenagers are 50 percent more susceptible to colds than are people over age 50.

The vagina and the eye are self-cleaning organs.

While sleeping, 1 man in 8 snores, and 1 in 10 grinds his teeth.

It's harder to tell a convincing lie to someone you find sexually attractive.

The average person produces about 12,000 gallons of urine over the course of a lifetime.

Anthropologists know of no human society whose children don't play hide-and-seek.

Male patients fall out of hospital beds twice as often as do female patients.

Airline Acronyms

AER LINGUS
Arousing Erotic Randy Ladies In Nice Green Uniform Suits

AEROFLOT
Aircraft Everywhere Run On Fuel Left Over by Tanks

AIR INDIA
An Interesting Ride, I'll Not Do It Again

ALITALIA
Always Late In Transit, Always Late In Arrival

AMERICAN
A Miracle Each Rider Is Currently Alive Now
Airline Meals Eaten Regularly Induce Cramps And Nausea

DELTA

> Departures Extra-Late, Tardy Arrivals
> Doesn't Even Leave The Airport

EL AL

> Every Landing
> Always Late
> Everyone's
> Luggage Always
> Lost

EMIRATES

> English Managed,
> Indian Run, A Thousand
> Ex-pats Suffering

FINNAIR

> Flies Ideally? Nah, Not
> Airborne In Reality

GULF AIR

> Get Used to Late Flights—Aircraft In Repair

KLM

> Kamikaze Loving Maniacs

LOT

> Lots Of Trouble

LUFTHANSA

> Let Us Fondle The Hostess And Not Say Anything

OLYMPIC

> Onassis Likes Your Money Paid In Cash

QANTAS

> Quick And Nasty Transportation,
> Australian Style
> Quite A Neat Trick, Arriving Safely
> Quits Air-travel, Next Time Approaches Ship

RYANAIR

> Running Your Ailing National
> Airline Into Receivership

SABENA

> Such A Bad Experience—
> Never Again

SAS

> Sex Always Supplied
> Same As Sabena

SWISSAIR

> Sexy Women In Swissair
> Service Are Incredibly
> Rare

UNITED

> Usually Not Inclined To
> Eliminate Disasters

VIRGIN

> Very Interesting Ride: Going Into Nowhere

Animals, Etc.

An elephant's trunk can hold 2 gallons of water.

> **An adult lion's roar** is so loud it can be heard up to 5
> miles away.

The word "rodent" comes from the Latin word *rodere,* meaning to gnaw.

> **A mole** can dig over 250 feet of tunnel in a single
> night.

A cow's only sweat glands are in its nose.

When a horned toad is angry, it squirts blood from its eyes.

The average gorilla has a penis that is 2 inches long.

Bats have sex in the air.

Chameleons can move their eyes independently: one eye can look forward at the same time as the other looks back.

The pocket gopher, a burrowing rodent, can run backward as fast as it can run forward.

A chamois goat can balance on a point of rock the size of a dollar coin.

Frogs don't drink water—they absorb it through their skin.

A giraffe's erect penis is 4 feet long.

Bulls and crocodiles are color-blind.

The ragdoll is the largest breed of domesticated cat in the world.

The sloth moves so slowly that green algae can grow undisturbed on its fur.

Male boars excite females by breathing on their faces.

The poison arrow frog has enough poison to kill 2,200 people.

Emus can't walk backward.

Pigs can cover a mile in 7.5 minutes when running at top speed.

Iguanas can and do commit suicide.

The giraffe has the highest blood pressure of any animal.

A crocodile's tongue is attached to the roof of its mouth.

Crocodiles swallow stones to help them dive deeper.

Gorillas sleep for up to 14 hours a day.

Giraffes can't cough.

The last of a cat's senses to develop is its sight.

The ancient Egyptians trained baboons to wait tables.

A woodchuck breathes only 10 times during hibernation.

Sloths spend 75 percent of their lives asleep.

Camels are born without humps.

Despite the hump, a camel's spine is straight.

Elephants sleep for about 2 hours per day.

Both crocodiles and cats can open and close their jaws but cannot move them side to side.

Armadillos can be house-trained.

Elephants are not afraid of mice.

Mice will nurse babies that are not their own.

The orangutan's warning signal to would-be aggressors is a loud belch.

During mating, the male Californian sea-otter grips the nose of the female with his teeth.

A giraffe's heart is 2 feet long.

Pumas can leap a distance of about 60 feet.

Crocodiles carry their young in their mouths.

A sloth can move twice as fast in water as it can on land.

A hippopotamus is born underwater.

A python is capable of devouring a pig whole.

Crocodiles cannot stick out their tongues.

A crocodile can run at speeds of 11 miles per hour.

A sow always has an even number of teats or nipples, usually 12.

"Hog" is a generic name for all swine—so a pig is a hog, but a hog is not necessarily a pig.

The distance between an alligator's eyes, in inches, is equivalent to its length in feet.

Horses and rabbits can't vomit.

A rat's performance in a maze can be improved by playing Mozart to it.

African heart-nosed bats have such a keen sense of hearing that they can hear the footsteps of a beetle on sand 6 feet away.

The pupils in goat's and sheep's eyes are rectangular.

A female ferret can die if she goes into heat and can't find a mate.

A hedgehog's heart beats 190 times a minute but drops to 20 beats per minute during hibernation.

Lions cannot roar until they reach the age of 2.

Male goats will pee on each other in order to attract mates.

All the pet hamsters in the world are descended from one female wild golden hamster found with a litter of 12 young in Syria in 1930.

The Argentinean horned toad can consume an entire mouse in one swallow.

Cows can hear lower and higher frequencies than we can.

Elephants walk on tiptoe— the back of the foot is made up of fat and no bone.

Human birth-control pills work on gorillas.

It takes a sloth up to 6 days to digest the food it eats.

A rhinoceros's horn is made of compacted hair.

A dog can suffer from tonsillitis but not appendicitis. It doesn't have an appendix.

An elephant has about 100 gallons of blood.

The average dairy cow produces 4 times its weight in manure each year.

Nose prints are the most reliable way to identify dogs.

A chimpanzee can learn to recognize itself in a mirror, but a monkey can't.

A polecat is not a cat. It is a nocturnal European weasel.

All cats step with both left legs, then both right legs, when they walk or run. The only other animals to do this are the giraffe and the camel.

Every known dog except the chow has a pink tongue—the chow's tongue is jet black.

Every year in the United States, more people are killed by deer than by any other animal.

Sex between snakes lasts from 6 to 12 hours.

The tenrac, a Madagascan insectivore, has 22 to 24 nipples.

The two-toed sloth is the only other animal (apart from humans) that mates face-to-face.

A mouse has more bones than a man: mouse 225, man 206.

Greyhounds can reach their top speed of 45 miles per hour in just three strides.

Cows and horses sleep standing up.

An elephant trunk has 40,000 muscles but no bone.

A giraffe has the same number of bones in its neck as a human has.

The South American giant anteater eats more than 30,000 ants a day.

The red kangaroo of Australia can leap 27 feet in one bound.

Beaver teeth are so sharp that Native Americans once used them as knife blades.

A grasshopper needs a minimum air temperature of 62 degrees Fahrenheit before it's able to hop.

An elephant can eat a quarter of a ton of grass in a day.

Being nearsighted, sometimes a moose will approach a car, thinking it is another moose.

Rabbits have been known to reach a speed of 47 miles per hour.

An iguana can stay underwater for 28 minutes.

Brand-new baby giraffes are 6 feet tall and weigh almost 200 pounds.

Moose intercourse typically lasts about 5 seconds.

Giraffes rarely sleep more than 20 minutes a day.

A cat has 32 muscles in each ear.

"Kangaroo" means "I don't understand" in Aborigine.

A polar bear's skin is black. Its fur is not white but clear.

Polar bear liver contains so much vitamin A that it could be fatal to a human.

Minks have sex that lasts about 8 hours.

A rat can fall from a five-story building without injury.

Greyhounds have the best eyesight of any dog.

When a giraffe is born, it has to fall around 6 feet to the ground.

The greater dwarf lemur in Madagascar always gives birth to triplets.

Sheep are mentioned 45 times and goats 88 times in the Bible.

The placement of a donkey's eyes in its head enables it to see all 4 feet at one time.

Camels have 3 eyelids to protect themselves from blowing sand.

Frogs and toads never eat with their eyes open because they have to push food down into their stomach with the back of their eyeballs.

Hamsters blink 1 eye at a time.

A chameleon's tongue is twice the length of its body.

Brazil, Argentina, Australia and New Zealand all have more cattle than people.

Australia, Uruguay, Syria and Bolivia all have more sheep than people.

Denmark has twice as many pigs as people.

Alaska has almost twice as many caribou as people.

Paris is said to have more dogs than people.

Giraffes have no vocal cords.

A full-grown bear can run as fast as a horse.

The cheetah is the only cat that can't retract its claws.

A rodent's teeth never stop growing.

Beavers can hold their breath for 45 minutes.

The skin of a hippopotamus is nearly bulletproof.

Birds, Etc.

Lyrebirds can imitate any sound they hear, from a car alarm to an electric chain saw.

The owl can't move its eyes, but it's the only creature able to turn its head in a complete circle.

Apart from chocolate and avocados, which are highly toxic to the parrot, pet parrots can eat most of the food we eat.

Kiwis are the only birds that hunt by smell.

A male emperor penguin spends 60 days or more protecting his mate's eggs, which he keeps on his feet, covered with a feathered flap. During this time he doesn't eat and loses about 25 pounds. When the chicks hatch, he feeds them a liquid from his throat. When the female penguin returns to care for the young, the male goes to sea to eat and rest.

The smallest bird in the world is the bee hummingbird: it's 2.24 inches long and weighs less than a dime.

The pouch under a pelican's bill holds up to 25 pounds of fish and water.

Geese often mate for life and can pine to death at the loss of their mate.

The kiwi is the only bird with nostrils at the end of its bill.

Penguins are the only bird that can leap into the air like a porpoise.

The shell constitutes 12 percent of an egg's weight.

Only the male nightingale sings.

The emu gets its name from the Portuguese word for "ostrich."

An eagle can kill a young deer and fly away with it.

Ostriches stick their heads in the sand to look for water.

There is a type of parrot in New Zealand that likes to eat the rubber strips that line car windows.

The fastest bird in the world is the peregrine falcon, which can fly faster than 200 miles per hour.

When the air force was conducting test runs and breaking the sound barrier, fields of turkeys dropped dead.

When the first duck-billed platypus arrived at the British Museum, the curators thought it was a fake and tried to pull its beak off.

A vulture will never attack a human or animal that is moving.

The albatross can sleep in flight.

A pigeon can't lay an egg unless she sees another pigeon. If another pigeon isn't available, her own reflection in a mirror will do.

It takes about 40 minutes to hard-boil an ostrich egg.

Fish, Etc.

A male catfish keeps the eggs of his young in his mouth until they are ready to hatch.

Sharks will continue to attack, even when disemboweled.

In order to mate, a male deepsea anglerfish will bite a female and never let go—eventually merging his body into hers and spending the rest of his life inside her.

The red mullet turns red only after death.

Many male fish blow bubbles when they want to mate.

Whales increase their weight 30 billion times in their first two years.

A large whale needs more than 2 tons of food a day.

The closest relative to the manatee is the elephant.

A dolphin's hearing is so acute that it can pick up an underwater sound from fifteen miles away.

When young, black sea basses are mostly female, but at the age of 5, many become male.

Whales can't swim backward.

To change its line of sight, a whale must move its entire body.

The walking catfish can live on land.

A baby oyster is called a spat.

If a lobster loses an eye, it can grow a new one.

A red sponge can be broken into a thousand pieces and still reconstitute itself.

The flounder, a flatfish, has both eyes on one side of its body.

One species of shark is so competitive that the babies fight each other within the womb, until only one is left to be born alive.

Bluefin tuna can swim at 50 miles per hour.

Sharks are immune to all known diseases.

The shrimp's heart is in its head.

Oysters can change from one gender to the other and back again.

Sharks will eat anything *except* something in the vicinity of where they give birth. This is the only way nature protects them from accidentally eating their own babies.

The European freshwater mussel lives for at least 90 years.

Five piranha fish could chew up a horse and rider in 7 minutes.

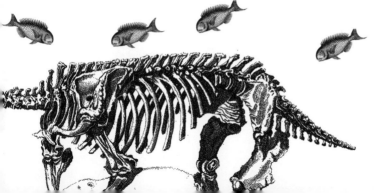

To keep from being separated while sleeping, sea otters tie themselves together with kelp.

A shark can grow a new set of teeth in a week.

A humpback whale's penis can be longer than 10 feet.

A whale can swim for 3 months without eating.

A whale's penis is called a dork.

Eighty-five percent of all life on Earth is plankton.

Turtles can live for more than 100 years.

At 188 decibels, the whistle of the blue whale is the loudest sound produced by any animal.

All clams start out as males; some become females later.

Insects, Etc.

A queen bee lays about 1,500 eggs a day.

The size of a mosquito penis is 1/100 of an inch.

The average bee yields only a twelfth of a teaspoon of honey in its life.

Bees flap their wings 11,400 times a minute.

A female mosquito can produce 150 million young in one year.

Some ribbon worms will eat bits of themselves if they can't find any food.

Insects shiver when they're cold.

After eating, a housefly regurgitates its food and then eats it again.

A butterfly warms up its body to 81 degrees Fahrenheit before flying.

The cicada, a fly found in Africa, spends 17 years of its life sleeping. In the two weeks it's awake, it mates and then dies.

A leech has 32 brains.

Earthworms have 5 hearts.

A snail has about 25,000 teeth.

Mosquitoes like the scent of estrogen, so women get bitten by mosquitoes more than men do.

A typical bed houses over 6 billion dust mites.

There are over 1,800 known species of flea.

The longest earthworm ever found was 22 feet long.

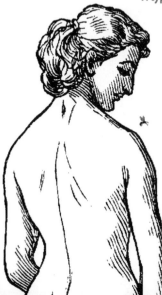

Mosquitoes are attracted to the color blue twice as much as to any other color.

A snail can crawl across a razor blade without getting injured because it excretes a protective slime.

Cockroaches can survive underwater for 15 minutes.

Australian termites have been known to build mounds 20 feet high and at least 100 feet wide.

Slugs have 4 noses.

If a cockroach breaks a leg, it can grow another one.

A spiderweb is a natural clotting agent; applied to a cut, it quickly stops the flow of blood.

The aphid's reproductive cycle is so fast that females are born pregnant.

The world's termites outweigh the world's humans 10 to 1.

Stag beetles have stronger mandibles than humans do.

More people are killed each year by bees than by snakes.

Adult earwigs can float in water for up to 24 hours.

The black widow spider can devour as many as 20 "mates" in a single day.

Bees are born fully grown.

In relation to its size, the ordinary house spider is 8 times faster than an Olympic sprinter.

The average garden snail has a top speed of 0.03 miles per hour.

Ants can't chew their food, so they move their jaws sideways to extract the juices from it.

Mexican jumping beans jump because of a moth larva inside the bean.

The creature with the largest brain in relation to its body is the ant.

The female praying mantis devours her partner while they're mating.

The sensors on the feet of a red admiral butterfly are 200 times more sensitive to sugar than the human tongue is.

A snail's reproductive organs are in its head.

Termites do more damage in the United States every year than all the fires, storms and earthquakes combined.

A mosquito has 47 teeth.

A dragonfly's penis has a shovel on the end that scoops out a rival male's semen.

Slugs can fertilize their own eggs.

Ants don't sleep.

Onlys

The bloodhound is the **only** animal whose evidence is admissible in an American court.

Monday is the **only** day of the week that has an anagram: dynamo.

Libra (the scales) is the only inanimate symbol in the zodiac.

The only countries in the world with one syllable in their English names are Chad, France, Greece and Spain.

The only rock that floats in water is pumice.

There wasn't a single pony in the Pony Express, only horses.

Malayalam, spoken in Kerala, southern India, is the only language with a palindromic name.

A person from the country of Nauru is called a Nauruan; this is the only palindromic nationality.

In Germany there's a flea that lives and breeds **only** in beer mats.

Almonds and pistachios are the **only** nuts mentioned in the Bible.

"Subbookkeeper" is the only word found in an English dictionary with four pairs of double letters in a row.

Only male turkeys (toms) gobble; females make a clicking noise.

"Forty" is the only number that has its letters in alphabetical order.

"One" is the only number with its letters in reverse alphabetical order.

The only Dutch word to contain eight consecutive consonants is angstschreeuw.

Your tongue is the only muscle in your body that is attached at only one end.

Only female mosquitoes bite, and only female mosquitoes buzz.

The only two people in the Baseball Hall of Fame who had nothing to do with baseball are Abbott and Costello.

No president of the United States was an only child.

If there were an ocean big enough, Saturn would be the only planet that could float, because its density is lighter than that of water (it is mostly gas).

Goethe could write only if he had an apple rotting in the drawer of his desk.

The only bone not broken so far in any ski accident is one located in the inner ear.

Rudyard Kipling wrote only in black ink.

The only person ever to decline a Pulitzer Prize for Fiction was Sinclair Lewis.

Hummingbirds are the only birds able to fly backward.

Christopher Lee was the only member of the cast (and crew) of the *Lord of the Rings* movies to have met J. R. R. Tolkien.

New Zealand is the only country that contains every type of climate in the world.

Pierre, the capital of South Dakota, is the only U.S. state capital name that shares no letters with the name of its state.

Earth is the only planet not named after a god.

Black lemurs are the only primates, other than humans, that can have blue eyes.

The Dutch town of Abcoude is the only town or city in the world whose name begins with *abc*.

Maine is the only U.S. state with just one syllable.

Maine is also the only U.S. state that borders **only** one other state.

Only two U.S. states have names beginning with double consonants: Florida and Rhode Island (if you don't count Wyoming).

Only two countries have borders on three oceans—the United States and Canada.

Europe is the only continent without a desert.

The letter w is the only letter in the alphabet that has three syllables—rather than one.

Theodore Roosevelt was the **only** U.S. president to deliver an inaugural address without using the word "I." (Abraham Lincoln, Franklin D. Roosevelt and Dwight D. Eisenhower tied for second place, using "I" **only** once in their inaugural addresses.)

Nauru is the only country in the world with no official capital.

Snails mate **only** once in a lifetime, but it can take up to 12 hours.

Lake Nicaragua boasts the only freshwater sharks in the world.

The **only** wild camels in the world are in Australia.

The Boston University Bridge (on Commonwealth Avenue, Boston, Massachusetts) is the only place in the United States where a boat can sail under a train going under a car driving under an airplane.

The polar bear is the **only** mammal with hair on the soles of its feet.

Early Greek and Roman physicians believed that the **only** way to grow a good crop of basil was to curse while scattering the seeds.

Pecans are the **only** food that astronauts can take untreated into space.

A Dalmatian is the only dog that can get gout.

A bowling pin has to tilt **only** 7.5 degrees to fall down.

General Robert E. Lee is the only person ever to have graduated from the West Point military academy without a single demerit.

Only two female mammals possess hymens: humans and horses.

Only two male mammals possess prostates: humans and dogs.

Brenda Fricker, Kerry Packer and Steven Spielberg have **only** one kidney each. (Mel Gibson has a horseshoe kidney—two kidneys fused into one.)

Things Said by W. C. Fields

"Start every day off with a smile and get it over with."

"I never vote for anyone; I always vote against."

"Say anything that you like about me except that I drink water."

"After two days in hospital, I took a turn for the nurse."

"I certainly don't drink all the time. I have to sleep, you know."

"Anybody who hates children and dogs can't be all bad."

"I exercise extreme self-control: I never drink anything stronger than gin before breakfast."

"**Women are like elephants to me;** they're nice to look at, but I wouldn't want to own one."

"Horse sense is the thing a horse has which keeps it from betting on people."

"**A thing worth having** is a thing worth cheating for."

"I've been on a diet for two weeks, and all I've lost is two weeks."

"**The funniest thing a comedian** can do is not do it."

"Once, during Prohibition, I was forced to live for days on nothing but food and water."

"**A rich man is nothing** but a poor man with money."

"Never give a sucker an even break."

"**I'm just looking for loopholes."** (when caught reading the Bible on his deathbed)

"On the whole, I'd rather be in Philadelphia." (his epitaph)

Pure Trivia, II

Amber was once thought to be solidified sunshine or the petrified tears of gods.

There are 1,929,770,126,028,800 different color combinations possible on a Rubik's Cube.

Cleopatra used pomegranate seeds for lipstick.

The decibel was named after Alexander Graham Bell.

"Honcho" comes from the Japanese word meaning "squad leader."

Mel Blanc, the voice of Bugs Bunny, was allergic to carrots.

English soldiers of the Hundred Years' War were known to the French as "Les Goddamns" because of their propensity to swear.

A cat falling from the seventh floor of a building has a 30 percent smaller chance of surviving than if it falls off the twentieth floor. It takes about eight floors for the cat to realize what's going on and prepare itself.

Hydrangeas produce pink and white flowers in alkaline soil and blue ones in acidic soil.

Rabbits love licorice.

Malaria was originally believed to be caused by the vapors rising from swamps (the name comes from words meaning "bad air").

Portland, Oregon, was named in a coin toss in 1844. Heads Portland, tails Boston.

Fifty percent of all marshmallows consumed in the United States have been toasted.

One superstition about how to get rid of warts is to rub them with a peeled apple and then feed the apple to a pig.

Traditionally a groom must carry a bride over the threshold to protect her from being possessed by the evil spirits that hang around in doorways.

The "live long and prosper" sign made by *Star Trek*'s Mr. Spock is the sign that Jewish priests (*cohenim*) used while saying certain prayers.

St. Cassian was a schoolmaster whose pupils stabbed him to death with their pens.

According to the ancient Chinese, swinging your arms cures headache pain.

Pliny believed that the souls of the dead resided in beans.

Coffee drinkers have sex more frequently and enjoy it more than non–coffee drinkers.

Ham radio operators got their name from the expression "ham-fisted operators," a term used to describe early radio users who sent Morse code (i.e., pounded their fists).

Syphilis was known as the French disease in Italy and the English disease in France.

Apples are more effective than caffeine at keeping people awake in the morning.

A can of Spam is opened every four seconds.

Lipstick contains fish scales.

Kidney stones come in a range of colors from yellow to brown.

A stretched-out Slinky is 87 feet long.

The hundred-billionth Crayola crayon was Periwinkle Blue.

Pinocchio was made of pine.

More people are killed annually by donkeys than in airplane crashes.

Maine is the toothpick capital of the world.

New Jersey has a spoon museum with over 5,400 spoons.

There was once a town in West Virginia called "6."

The colder the room you sleep in, the more likely you are to have a bad dream.

The Gulf Stream would carry a message in a bottle at an average of 4 miles per hour.

The monkey wrench was invented by Charles Moncke.

Before Fame

Noel Gallagher used to be a roadie for the Inspiral Carpets (and Liam got the name Oasis from an Inspiral Carpets poster).

Catherine Zeta-Jones broke into show business as a teenage Shirley Bassey impersonator. Her father drove her around the workingmen's clubs to perform.

Geena Davis has an elbow that bends the wrong way (and when she was young, she'd do things like stand in an elevator and, when the doors would close, pretend that her arm had got caught).

Fidel Castro was voted Cuba's best schoolboy athlete (in 1944).

Axl Rose used to earn eight dollars an hour for smoking cigarettes (in a science experiment at UCLA).

Emma Bunton played one of the bridesmaids catapulted onto a giant wedding cake in a Halifax Building Society TV commercial.

Michelle Pfeiffer used to be a clerk at Von's grocery store in California. While there, she learned to tie cherry stems in knots with her tongue.

Michael Crichton handed in a paper written by George Orwell to see if his college professor had something against him. He got a B–.

Matt Damon used to break-dance for money in Harvard Square.

> **Oprah Winfrey** once approached Aretha Franklin as she got out of a limo and convinced the singer that she was abandoned. Aretha gave her a hundred dollars, which she used to stay in a hotel.

Former Altar Boys

Pierce Brosnan, Phil Donahue, Michael Gambon, Neil Jordan, Martin Scorsese, Louis Farrakhan, Bob Guccione, Bernhard Langer, Oliver North, Engelbert Humperdinck

Dropped Out of College

Ben Affleck (two colleges), Beau Bridges, Vin Diesel, Bill Murray, Dennis Quaid, Steven Spielberg, Stephen Stills, Eric Stoltz, Paula Abdul, Courteney Cox, Rosie O'Donnell, Marisa Tomei, Kate Beckinsale

Spent Part of Their Childhood in a Brothel

James Brown

Louis Armstrong

Chico Marx (played piano in one)

Harpo Marx (also played piano but knew only two songs, which he played over and over again at different speeds)

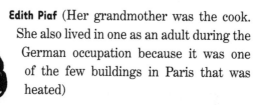

Edith Piaf (Her grandmother was the cook. She also lived in one as an adult during the German occupation because it was one of the few buildings in Paris that was heated)

Richard Pryor (his grandmother was the owner)

N.B.: Henri de Toulouse-Lautrec lived in a brothel as an adult

Attended Art School

Robbie Coltrane, Ralph Fiennes, Jonathan Pryce, Bryan Ferry, David Byrne, John Lennon, Sofia Coppola, Jim Broadbent

Teenage Runaways

Courtney Love, Oprah Winfrey, Bob Dylan, Daniel Day-Lewis, Billy Connolly, Errol Flynn, Pierce Brosnan, Cary Grant, Ella Fitzgerald

Rhodes Scholars

Bill Clinton, Bill Bradley, Kris Kristofferson, Bob Hawke, Terrence Malick, Naomi Wolf, David Kirk, Dom Mintoff, Edward de Bono, Carl Albert, J. William Fulbright, Robert Penn Warren, Dean Rusk, General Wesley Clark

Attended the Sorbonne

Alan Alda, Jean-Luc Godard, Sam Waterston, Jacqueline Kennedy Onassis, Rose Tremain, Verity Lambert, Christian Lacroix, Liza Minnelli

Former Cheerleaders

Reese Witherspoon, Meryl Streep, Paula Abdul, Madonna, Sally Field, Raquel Welch, Carly Simon, Jerry Lewis, Angela Bassett, Sandra Bullock, Renée Zellweger (star cheerleader), Cameron Diaz, Charisma Carpenter (for the

San Diego Chargers), Steve Martin, Alicia Silverstone, Calista Flockhart, Jack Lemmon, Sela Ward, Teri Hatcher (for the San Francisco 49ers), Kirsten Dunst

N.B.: Uma Thurman abandoned her dreams of becoming a cheerleader at the age of ten after a bad experience at summer camp. "The players were kind of embarrassed. We certainly didn't turn them on."

Former Boy Scouts

Bill Clinton, Mark Spitz, Richard Gere, Derek Jacobi, Neil Armstrong, Jacques Chirac, Jeffrey Archer, Jason Donovan, Roger Rees, James Stewart, Richard Attenborough, Edward Woodward, Keith Richards, George Michael, Paul McCartney

Former Girl Guides/Scouts

Björk, Emma Thompson, Margaret Thatcher, Mariah Carey, Princess Margaret, Venus Williams, Glenda Jackson, Princess Anne, Queen Elizabeth II, Natasha Richardson, Hillary Clinton, Belinda Carlisle, Kate Moss

Homecoming Queens

Rosie O'Donnell, Sela Ward, Caprice, Meryl Streep, Sissy Spacek, Meg Ryan, Lynne Cheney, Barbara Bush (Dubya's daughter), Kay Hartenstein, Tori Amos, Elizabeth Dole, Nicole Brown (O. J. Simpson's ex-wife), Sharon Tate

Achievements Before the Age of 10

At the age of 3, Elizabeth Taylor danced in front of King George V.

At the age of 3, the nineteenth-century English philosopher John Stuart Mill was able to read Greek.

At the age of 5, Natalie Wood appeared in her first film.

At the age of 5, Tori Amos won a scholarship to study piano in a Baltimore conservatory (but was kicked out by the age of 11).

At the age of 6, Shirley Temple was awarded an honorary Oscar "in grateful recognition of her outstanding contribution to screen entertainment during the year 1934."

At the age of 7, Fred Astaire was performing in vaudeville.

At the age of 9, Macaulay Culkin was cast as the lead character in *Home Alone*, the movie that made him famous.

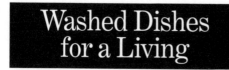

Washed Dishes for a Living

Ronald Reagan, Jacques Chirac, Burt Reynolds, Roseanne, Little Richard, Roger Moore, Chrissie Hynde, Uma Thurman, Warren Beatty, Dustin Hoffman, Carlos Santana, Robert Duvall

Trained as Commercial Artists

David Bowie, Bob Hoskins, Dirk Bogarde, Gene Hackman, Pete Townshend

Worked as Ushers

Sylvester Stallone, Barbra Streisand, Charlene Tilton, George Michael, George Segal, Kirk Douglas, Heather Graham, Al Pacino, Joseph Fiennes (and once told off Helen Mirren for not sitting down without realizing that she was one of the actresses)

Worked as Models

Joaquin Phoenix, Sharon Stone, Jessica Biel, Penelope Cruz, Bijou Phillips, Denise Richards, Chloe Sevigny, Mena Suvari, Christopher Walken, Emily Watson (for Laura Ashley, age 4), Willem Dafoe, Ashton Kutcher, Brooke Shields, Jacqueline Bisset, Sylvia Kristel, Gerald Ford, Ali MacGraw, Charlotte Rampling, George Lazenby, Ellen Burstyn, Burt Reynolds, Jessica Lange, Dyan Cannon, Courteney Cox, Ted Danson, Susan Dey, Farrah Fawcett, Tom Selleck, Cybill Shepherd, Antonio Banderas, Cameron Diaz, Nick Nolte, Lindsay Lohan (age 3)

Started Out as Extras

Dustin Hoffman, Marilyn Monroe, Ronald Reagan, Clint Eastwood, Donald Sutherland, John Wayne, Robert De Niro, Bill Cosby, Clark Gable, Robert Duvall, Gary Cooper, Marlene Dietrich, Paulette Goddard, Stewart Granger, Jean Harlow, Sophia Loren, David Niven, Rudolph Valentino, Cate Blanchett (when she was 18, in a boxing movie filmed in Egypt where she was vacationing. She appeared in a crowd scene cheering for an American boxer who was losing to an Egyptian; she hated it so much she walked off the set), Gary Sinise (in *General Hospital*), Phil Collins (in *A Hard Day's Night*), Ben Affleck and Matt Damon (in *Field of Dreams*).

Served in Korea

Neil Armstrong, Michael Caine, Frank Gorshin (as an entertainer), James Garner, Ty Hardin, Screamin' Jay Hawkins, Lee Hazlewood, Ed McMahon, Jamie Farr (Corporal Klinger in the TV series *M*A*S*H*—the only member of the cast to have served in Korea), Faron Young, Berry Gordy Jr., Charlie Rich, Link Wray, Leonard Nimoy, Robert Duvall

Served in Vietnam

Oliver Stone, Al Gore, Steve Kanaly (awarded the Purple Heart for the injuries he suffered there), Charles Lindbergh (as a brigadier general), Oliver North, Colin Powell (two tours; awarded the Purple Heart), Dennis Franz (eleven months in an elite airborne division), Brian Dennehy (was in the marines for over five years and served eight months in Vietnam before returning home with shrapnel wounds and a concussion), Wesley Clark (was shot; awarded Silver Star for bravery), James Avery, Troy Evans

Stephen King failed the medical exam on four counts: flat feet, limited vision, high blood pressure and a punctured eardrum.

Roger Ebert went to the draft for the Vietnam War but was rejected for being overweight. He was 26 years old and weighed 206 pounds.

Micky Dolenz was drafted to serve in the U.S. Army in 1967 despite medical grounds for deferment—trouble with Perthese disease in childhood had left him with one leg shorter than the other. Dolenz was eventually excused from military service for being underweight. Davy Jones was also drafted but was excused as his family's sole source of support.

Conscientious Objectors

Carl Wilson, Muhammad Ali, Richard Dreyfuss, Lew Ayres, Donald Pleasence (although he later joined up), Fritz Weaver

Mickey Mouse Club "Mouseketeers"

Justin Timberlake, Christina Aguilera, Britney Spears, J. C. Chasez, Keri Russell

Studied to Be Architects

Art Garfunkel, Rifat Ozbek, Queen Noor of Jordan, Carla Bruni, Chris Lowe, Roger Waters

Lived on a Kibbutz

Sacha Baron Cohen (Ali G.), Sigourney Weaver, Isla Fisher, Annie Leibovitz, Bob Hoskins, Mike Leigh, Uri Geller, Dr. Ruth Westheimer

Qualified Medical Doctors

Che Guevara, Graham Chapman, Anton Chekhov, Michael Crichton

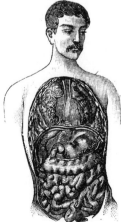

Worked in the Circus

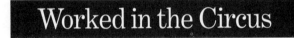

Pierce Brosnan (fire-eater in his teens)

Roberto Benigni (clown)

Christopher Walken (assistant lion tamer)

Harry Houdini (escapologist)

Burt Lancaster (acrobat)

Bob Hoskins (fire-eater)

Rupert Graves (clown)

W. C. Fields (elephant attendant)

Yul Brynner (trapeze artist)

Left-Handed

Sarah Jessica Parker, Jean-Paul Gaultier, Angelina Jolie, Drew Barrymore, Eminem, Bruce Willis, Demi Moore, Goldie Hawn, Bobby Charlton, Shirley MacLaine, Phil Mickelson, Diane Keaton, Robert De Niro, Emma Thompson, Matthew Broderick, Ringo Starr, George Michael, Tom Cruise, Richard Dreyfuss, Robert Redford, Bob Geldof, Mark Spitz, Jennifer Saunders, Phil Collins, Oprah Winfrey, Julia Roberts, Ryan O'Neal, Prince William, Bill Clinton, Uri Geller, George H. W. Bush, Paul McCartney, Terence Stamp, Seal

Unfortunately Named Products and Campaigns

Parker Pens' slogan "Avoid embarrassment—use Quink," when translated into Spanish came out as "Avoid pregnancy—use Quink."

Plessey and **GEC** had a joint company in France called GPT. When this is pronounced in French, it comes out as Jay-Pay-Tay, which sounds like *J'ai pète*, meaning "I have farted."

Mitsubishi launched its Pajero 4WD in Spanish-speaking territories without realizing that "pajero" is Spanish for "jerk."

The computer company Wang ran an Australian TV commercial that contained the slogan, "Wang cares." It ran for just the one day.

KFC's "finger-lickin' good" slogan was translated into China as "eat your fingers off."

Ford's car, the Pinto, couldn't be sold in Brazil because the word pinto is slang for a small penis.

Electrolux was obliged to abandon its slogan "Nothing sucks like Electrolux."

Coors had a slogan "Turn it loose," which, when translated into Spanish, became "suffer from diarrhea."

Pepsi-Cola had a slogan "Come alive with the Pepsi generation," which, when translated into Chinese, became "Pepsi brings your ancestors back from the grave."

Similarly, the name Coca-Cola was at first Ke-kou-ke-la in Chinese, until the company discovered that the phrase means "bite the wax tadpole" or "female horse stuffed with wax," depending on the dialect.

The Rolls-Royce Silver Mist line had to be renamed for the Germany market because mist means "dung" in German.

Puffs tissues didn't sell well in Germany because puff in German means "brothel."

The German hardware store chain Götzen opened a mall in Turkey but had to change the name as göt means "bum" in Turkish.

The Italian mineral water Traficante means "drug dealer" in Spanish.

Honda launched its new car the Fitta in Scandinavia—only to find that fitta was a slang word for "vagina" in Swedish, Norwegian and Danish.

Ford's Comet was called the Ford Caliente in Mexico, but although caliente literally means hot (as in temperature), it's also used colloquially as "horny." Ford had a similar problem in Latin American countries with their Fiera, which means "ugly old woman" there.

Hunt-Wesson introduced its Big John products in French Canada as Gros Jos before discovering that this is a slang expression for "big breasts."

When Mazda launched the Laputa, they didn't take into account the fact that puta is the Spanish word for "prostitute." The ads claiming that "Laputa is designed to deliver maximum utility in a minimum space while providing a smooth, comfortable ride" took on a new meaning.

A Nike TV commercial for hiking shoes was shot in Kenya using Samburu tribesmen, one of whom was caught mouthing—in native Maa—"I don't want these. Give me big shoes."

Nissan launched the Moco before discovering that moco is the Spanish for "mucus."

Perdue Chicken was advertised in Mexico with the slogan "It takes a tough man to make a tender chicken." When translated into Spanish, this became "It takes a hard man to make a chicken aroused."

The American slogan for Salem cigarettes, "Salem—Feeling Free," was translated into Japanese as "When smoking Salem, you feel so refreshed that your mind seems to be free and empty."

Samarin, a Swedish remedy for upset stomachs, ran an ad that was a series of three pictures. The first was of a man looking sick, the second was of him drinking a glass of Samarin, and the third was of him smiling. The company ran the ad in Arabic newspapers—where people read from right to left.

Toyota launched its MR2 model without realizing that, in France, it would be pronounced "em-er-deux," which sounds very similar to merde, meaning "shit."

Bacardi brought out a fruit drink that they named "Pavian" to suggest French chic, but, alas, pavian means "baboon" in German.

When Gerber first started selling baby food in Africa, they used their standard packaging with the cute baby on the label. Unfortunately, they were obliged to change it when they discovered that, in Africa, the standard practice is to put pictures of the contents on foods.

Jolly Green Giant translated into Arabic means "Intimidating Green Ogre."

When Braniff boasted about its seats in Spanish, what should have read "Fly in leather" became "Fly naked."

Geography

The Red Sea is not red.

China uses 45 billion chopsticks per year.

The Pacific Ocean covers 28 percent of the Earth's surface.

The poorest country in the world is Mozambique. (Switzerland is the richest.)

At the nearest point, Russia and America are less than 2.5 miles apart.

Alaska is the most northern, western and eastern state; it also has the highest latitude, the most eastern longitude and the most western longitude, and could hold the 21 smallest states.

Mongolia is the largest landlocked country.

The coastline of Alaska is longer than the entire coastline of the rest of the United States (excluding Hawaii).

Despite having a landmass over 27 times smaller, Norway's total coastline is longer than the United States.

The East Alligator River in Australia's Northern Territory harbors crocodiles, not alligators.

La Paz in Bolivia is so high above sea level there is barely enough oxygen in the air to support a fire.

Antarctic means "opposite the Arctic."

Less than 1 percent of the Caribbean Islands is inhabited.

The volume of water in the Amazon River is greater than the next 8 largest rivers in the world combined.

There is no point in England more than 75 miles from the sea.

Seoul, the South Korean capital, means "the capital" in the Korean language.

If an Amish man has a beard, he's married.

Parsley is the most widely used herb in the world.

Coca-Cola is Africa's largest private-sector employer.

The Coca-Cola company is the largest consumer of sugar in the world.

In Albania, nodding the head means "no" and shaking the head means "yes."

The people of Iceland read more books per capita than any other people in the world.

Eskimos use refrigerators to keep their food from freezing.

Two-thirds of the world's eggplants are grown in New Jersey.

Twenty-eight percent of Africa is wilderness; 38 percent of North America is wilderness.

The University of Alaska covers 4 time zones.

Approximately 20 percent of Americans have passports.

Canada has more lakes than the rest of the world combined.

One-third of all the fresh water on Earth is in Canada.

Ten percent of the salt mined in the world each year is used to de-ice the roads in America.

Own/Owned Islands

Marlon Brando (Tetiaroa)

Richard Branson (Necker)

Charles Haughey (Inis Mhicileain)

Björn Borg (Kattilo)

Malcolm Forbes (Lacaula)

Nick Faldo (Bartrath)

Björk (Ellidaey—given to her by the Icelandic government)

History

The first known contraceptive was crocodile dung, used by the Egyptians in 2000 B.C.

 **Armored knights** raised their visors to identify themselves when they rode past their king. This custom has become the modern military salute.

Nobody knows where Mozart is buried.

In the latter part of the eighteenth century, Prussian surgeons treated stutterers by snipping off portions of their tongues.

From 1807 till 1821, the capital of Portugal was moved to Rio de Janeiro, Brazil (at the time a colony of Portugal), while Portugal was fighting France in the Napoleonic Wars.

Abdul Kassem Ismael, the grand vizier of Persia in the tenth century, carried his library with him wherever he went. The 117,000 volumes were carried in alphabetical order by 400 camels.

Ethelred the Unready, king of England in the tenth century, spent his wedding night in bed with his wife and his mother-in-law.

The lance ceased to be an official battle weapon of the British Army in 1927.

The Toltecs, seventh-century native Mexicans, went into battle with wooden swords so as not to kill their enemies.

China banned the pigtail in 1911, as it was seen to be a symbol of feudalism.

During World War I, the future Pope John XXIII was a sergeant in the Italian army.

Emperor Caligula once decided to go to war against the Roman god of the sea, Poseidon, and ordered his soldiers to throw their spears into the water.

Between the two world wars, France was controlled by 40 different governments.

In 1939 the American Nazi Party had 200,000 members.

Richard II died in 1400. A hole was left in the side of his tomb so people could touch his royal head, but 376 years later someone stole his jawbone.

Albert Einstein was once offered the presidency of Israel. He declined, saying he had no head for problems.

Instant coffee has been around since the eighteenth century.

In medieval days Welsh mercenary bowmen wore one shoe at a time.

In about 1597, William Shakespeare gave *The Merry Wives of Windsor* to Queen Elizabeth I for Christmas because she wanted to see a play that featured Falstaff in love.

The river Nile has frozen over only twice—once in the ninth century and again in the eleventh century.

In ancient Egypt, if a patient died during an operation, the surgeon's hands were cut off.

In ancient China, doctors got paid only if the patient stayed in good health. If the patient's health deteriorated, sometimes the doctor had to pay him.

The Incas and the Aztecs were able to function without the wheel.

Alfred Nobel invented dynamite; his father, Emmanuel, invented plywood.

Roman emperor Caligula made his horse a senator.

In Sweden in the Middle Ages, a mayor was once elected by a louse. The candidates rested their beards on a table and the louse was placed in the middle. The louse's chosen host became mayor.

In ancient Egypt, when a cat died, it was mandatory for its owner to shave off his eyebrows to show his grief.

The ancient Celts believed that rivers were the urine of goddesses. Many European rivers (Seine, Severn, Danube, etc.) were named after these urinating Celtic deities.

Legend has it that after he was beheaded, St. Denis, the patron saint of Paris, carried his head around and walked for some distance.

During World War II, the American automobile industry produced just 139 cars.

The imperial throne of Japan has been occupied by the same family for the last 1,300 years.

During the crusades the difficulty of transporting bodies off the battlefield for burial was resolved by taking a huge cauldron onto the battlefield, boiling down the bodies and taking away the bones.

Homosexuality remained on the American Psychiatric Association's list of mental illnesses until 1973.

Spanish doubloons were legal tender in the United States until 1857.

Virginia Woolf and Lewis Carroll wrote their books standing up.

The Pentagon has twice as many toilets as necessary because in the 1940s, when it was built, the state of Virginia still had segregation laws requiring separate facilities for blacks and whites.

Between 1839 and 1855, Nicaragua had 396 different rulers.

Sultan Murad IV inherited 240 wives when he assumed the throne of Turkey in 1744. He put each wife into a sack and tossed them one by one into the Bosphorus.

During World War II, it was against the law in Germany to name a horse Adolf.

Napoleon constructed his battle plans in a sandbox.

Ancient Egyptians slept on pillows of stone.

The Egyptians thought it was good luck to enter a house left foot first.

Mark Twain was born on a day in 1835 when Halley's comet came into view. When he died in 1910, Halley's comet came into view again.

Louis XIV took just three baths in his lifetime (and he had to be coerced into taking those).

George I, king of England from 1714 to 1727, was German and couldn't speak a word of English.

In ancient Greece, tossing an apple to a girl was a traditional proposal of marriage. Catching it meant she accepted.

1 out of 25 coffins from the sixteenth century has been found to have scratch marks on the inside.

Gold

There is 200 times more gold in the world's oceans than has ever been mined.

All the gold ever mined would be as big as a three-bedroom house; all the gold that's still to be mined (on land) would only be big enough to make the garage.

Gold is the only metal that doesn't rust—even if it's buried in the ground for thousands of years.

India is the world's largest consumer of gold.

There are just 6 grams of gold in an Olympic Gold medal.

N.B.: In the original story of Cinderella, her slippers were made of gold, not glass. And her stepsisters were beautiful on the outside—their ugliness lay within.

Would Have Turned 100 in 2006

Carol Reed, British film director

Oscar Levant, American musician

Leonid Brezhnev, Russian politician

Otto Preminger, American film director

Hermione Baddeley, British actress

Louise Brooks, American actress

Luchino Visconti, Italian film director

Primo Carnera, American boxer

Janet Gaynor, American actress

Dmitri Shostakovich, Russian composer

Aristotle Onassis, Greek shipping billionaire

John Betjeman, British poet

Joan Blondell, American actress

Joan Hickson, British actress

John Huston, American film director

Clifford Odets, American playwright

Catherine Cookson, British writer

Billy Wilder, American film director

Josephine Baker, American singer

Libby Holman, American singer

Mary Astor, American actress

Roberto Rossellini, Italian film director

Samuel Beckett, Irish playwright

Henny Youngman, American comedian

Lou Costello, American comedian

Bugsy Siegel, American gangster

Madeleine Carroll, British actress

John Carradine, American actor

Dietrich Bonhoeffer, German clergyman

Lon Chaney Jr., American actor

Turn 90 in 2006

Olivia de Havilland, American actress

Kirk Douglas, American actor

Richard Fleischer, American film director

Walter Cronkite, American TV anchorman

June Havoc, Canadian actress

Van Johnson, American actor

Robert McNamara, American politician

Glenn Ford, American actor

Would Have Turned 90 in 2006

Dinah Shore, American singer and TV star

Raf Vallone, American actor

Jackie Gleason, American actor

Harry James, American musician

Maxene Andrews, American singer

Mercedes McCambridge, American actress

Sterling Hayden, American actor

Irwin Allen, American writer/producer

Irene Worth, American actress

Harold Robbins, American writer

Margaret Lockwood, British actress

Keenan Wynn, American actor

James Herriot, British writer

Rossano Brazzi, Italian singer and actor

Edward Heath, British politician

Dick Haymes, Argentinian singer and actor

Ray Conniff, American musician

Yehudi Menuhin, British musician

Gregory Peck, American actor

Irving Wallace, American writer

Francis Crick, British scientist

Harold Wilson, British politician

Roald Dahl, British writer

François Mitterrand, French politician

Peter Finch, British actor

Betty Grable, American actress

Turn 80 in 2006

Frank Finlay, British actor

Tony Bennett, American singer

Queen Elizabeth II, British monarch

George Martin, British music producer

Lionel Jeffries, British actor

Alan Greenspan, American economist

Norman Jewison, Canadian film director

Bryan Forbes, British writer, actor and director

David Attenborough, British natural historian

Don Rickles, American comedian

Valery Giscard d'Estaing, French politician

Moira Shearer, British ballerina

Leslie Nielsen, Canadian actor

Beryl Cook, British artist

Hugh Hefner, American publisher

Chuck Berry, American singer/songwriter

Mel Brooks, American actor, writer and director

Jack Brabham, Australian racing driver

June Haver, American actress

Jeane Kirkpatrick, American diplomat

Joan Sutherland, Australian singer

Harry Dean Stanton, American actor

Peter Graves, American actor

Andrzej Wajda, Polish film director

Buddy Greco, American singer

Peter Shaffer, British playwright

Irene Papas, Greek actress

Bud Yorkin, American film director

Soupy Sales, American TV personality

Dr. Garret Fitzgerald, Irish politician

Shelley Berman, American comedian

Stuart Whitman, American actor

Clive Donner, British film director

Andy Griffith, American actor

Maria Schell, Austrian actress

J. P. Donleavy, Irish writer

Harper Lee, American writer

Would Have Turned
80 in 2006

Patricia Neal, American actress

Richard Crenna, American actor

Neal Cassady, American Beat Generation icon

Leonard Rossiter, British actor

John Coltrane, American musician

Klaus Kinski, German actor

Richard Jaeckel, American actor

Evan Hunter, American writer

Jeffrey Hunter, American actor

Karel Reisz, British film director

Fred Gwynne, American actor

H. R. Haldeman, American political aide

Steve Reeves, American actor

Anthony Shaffer, British playwright

Aldo Ray, American actor

Virgil "Gus" Grissom, American astronaut

Eric Morecambe, British comedian

John Derek, American actor

Marilyn Monroe, American actress

John Schlesinger, British film director

Kenneth Williams, British actor

Allen Ginsberg, American poet

Victor Kiam, American businessman

Miles Davis, American musician

Turn 70 in 2006

Alan Alda, American actor

Princess Alexandra, British royal

The Aga Khan

David Carradine, American actor

Gary Hart, American politician

Tommy Steele, British entertainer

Louis Gossett Jr., American actor

Dennis Hopper, American actor

Elizabeth Dole, American politician

Yves Saint Laurent, French fashion designer

Mary Tyler Moore, American actress

John Poindexter, American sailor

Bill Wyman, British musician

Roy Emerson, Australian tennis player

David Brenner, American comedian

Burt Reynolds, American actor

Tony O'Reilly, Irish businessman

Zubin Mehta, Indian orchestral conductor

Engelbert Humperdinck, British singer

Albert Finney, British actor

Glenda Jackson, British actress and politician

Sally Kellerman, American actress

A. S. Byatt, British writer

Hugh Hudson, British film director

Bruce Dern, American actor

Levi Stubbs, American singer

Richard Rodney Bennett, British composer

F. W. de Klerk, South African politician

Ursula Andress, Swiss actress

Glen Campbell, American singer

Dean Stockwell, American actor

Marion Barry, American politician

Joe Don Baker, American actor

Stella Stevens, American actress

Winnie Mandela, South African politician

Vaclav Havel, Czech playwright and politician

Anna Quayle, British actress

Rona Barrett, American news correspondent

Jim Brown, American football player and actor

Hugh Whitemore, British playwright

James Darren, American actor

Chad Everett, American actor

Kris Kristofferson, American actor and singer/songwriter

Buddy Guy, American musician

Ken Loach, British film director

Keir Dullea, American actor

Shirley Knight, American actress

Kenneth Mars, American actor

Would Have Turned 70 in 2006

Troy Donahue, American actor

Ismail Merchant, Indian film producer

Jill Ireland, British actress

Nyree Dawn Porter, New Zealander actress

Peter Tinniswood, British writer

Roy Orbison, American singer

Buddy Holly, American singer/songwriter

Wilt Chamberlain, American basketball player

Juliet Prowse, American actress and dancer

Bobby Darin, American actor and singer

Jim Henson, American puppeteer

Jim Clark, British racing driver

Michael Landon, American actor

Roger Miller, American singer

Turn 60 in 2006

Peter Wolf, American singer

Tim Curry, British actor

King Carl Gustaf of Sweden

Joanna Lumley, British actress

John Woo, Chinese film director

Lesley Gore, American singer

John Watson, British racing driver

Candice Bergen, American actress

Donovan, British singer/songwriter

Blair Brown, American actress

Talia Shire, American actress

John Waters, American film director

Ed O'Neill, American actor

Paul Schrader, American film director

Danny Glover, American actor

Ilie Nastase, Romanian tennis player

Bill Forsyth, British film director

Al Green, American singer

Loni Anderson, American actress

Susan Saint James, American actress

Jimmy Webb, American songwriter

Lesley Ann Warren, American actress

Bill Clinton, American politician

Connie Chung, American TV journalist

Hayley Mills, British actress

Jane Asher, British actress

Naomi Judd, American singer

John Paul Jones, British rock musician

Alan Rickman, British actor

Tyne Daly, American actress

Michael Radford, British film director

Malcolm McLaren, British rock-group manager

Lynda La Plante, British writer

Susan Sarandon, American actress

Charles Dance, British actor

Chris Tarrant, British DJ and TV host

Ben Vereen, American actor

Richard Carpenter, American musician

Suzanne Somers, American actress

Liza Minnelli, American actress and singer

Steve Kanaly, American actor

Ruth Pointer, American singer

Ron Silver, American actor/director and political activist

Sylvester Stallone, American actor

George W. Bush, American politician

Sue Lyon, American actress

Cheech Marin, American comedian

Linda Ronstadt, American singer

The Sultan of Brunei

Timothy Dalton, British actor

Bonnie Bedelia, American actress

Oliver Stone, American film director

Tommy Lee Jones, American actor

Bruce Davison, American actor

Donald Trump, American businessman

Marisa Berenson, American actress

Sally Field, American actress

Marianne Faithfull, British singer

Patti Smith, American singer/songwriter

Hubert Green, American golfer

Edgar Winter, American musician

Cher, American actress and singer

Brian Cox, British actor

Lasse Hallström, Swedish film director

Brenda Blethyn, British actress

Bob Beamon, American athlete

Barry Gibb, British-born singer/songwriter

Billy Preston, American musician

Buddy Miles, American musician

Loudon Wainwright III, American singer/songwriter

Sandy Duncan, American actress

Michael Ontkean, Canadian actor

Victoria Principal, American actress

Stephen Rea, Irish actor

José Carreras, Spanish singer

Diana Quick, British actress

Jimmy Buffett, American singer

Emerson Fittipaldi, Brazilian racing driver

Patty Duke, American actress

Michael Ovitz, American film mogul

Stan Smith, American tennis player

Carmine Appice, American musician

Benny Andersson, Swedish musician

Eugene Levy, Canadian actor and comedian

Steven Spielberg, American film director

Uri Geller, Israeli spoon bender

John Spencer, American actor

Josh Mostel, American actor

Gilbert O'Sullivan, Irish singer

Ivan Reitman, American film director

Peter Green, British musician

Alan Jones, Australian racing driver

Diane Keaton, American actress

Jann Wenner, American publisher

Robby Krieger, American musician

Dolly Parton, American singer

David Lynch, American film director

89

Would Have Turned 60 in 2006

Mick Ronson, British musician

Carrie Snodgress, American actress

Sanjay Gandhi, Indian politician

Gilda Radner, American actress

Keith Moon, British musician

Robert Urich, American actor

Gene Siskel, American film critic

Arthur Conley, American singer

Gianni Versace, Italian fashion designer

Duane Allman, American musician

Gregory Hines, American actor and dancer

Freddie Mercury, British singer

Ted Bundy, American serial killer

Gram Parsons, American singer/songwriter

Syreeta, American singer

Carl Wilson, American musician

Andrea Dworkin, American academic and writer

Turn 50 in 2006

Sugar Ray Leonard, American boxer

LaToya Jackson, American singer

Lisa Hartman, American actress

Björn Borg, Swedish tennis player

Kenny G, American singer/songwriter

Ingemar Stenmark, Swedish skier

Lena Olin, Swedish actress

Joan Allen, American actress

Kim Cattrall, American actress

Gerry Cooney, American boxer

Michael Feinstein, American musician

Stefan Johansson, Swedish racing driver

Joni Sledge, American singer

David Copperfield, American magician

Timothy Daly, American actor

Mel Gibson, Australian actor

David Caruso, American actor

Paul King, British rock musician

Shawn Colvin, American singer/songwriter

Phyllis Logan, British actress

Paul Young, British singer

Mimi Rogers, American actress

Geena Davis, American actress

Johnny Rotten/Lydon, British singer

Nathan Lane, American actor

Andy Garcia, American actor

Kevin McNally, British actor

Chris Isaak, American singer

Patricia Cornwell, American writer

Joe Montana, American football player

Anthony Bourdain, American chef

Jerry Hall, American model

Montel Williams, American talk-show host

Anita Hill, American lawyer

Dwight Yoakam, American country singer

Sinbad, American comedian and actor

Nigel Kennedy, British musician

Bo Derek, American actress

Michele Alboreto, Italian racing driver

Mickey Rourke, American actor

Rita Rudner, American comedienne

Debby Boone, American singer

Tom Hanks, American actor

Sela Ward, American actress

Michael Spinks, American boxer

Linda Hamilton, American actress

Carrie Fisher, American actress and writer

Martina Navratilova, Czech-born tennis player

Sebastian Coe, British athlete

Amanda Burton, British actress

Stephanie Zimbalist, American actress

Turn 40 in 2006

Jon Favreau, American actor/writer

Robin Wright Penn, American actress

Cynthia Nixon, American actress

Matthew Fox, American actor

Romario, Brazilian footballer

Stefan Edberg, Swedish tennis player

José Maria Olazabal, Spanish golfer

Rick Astley, British singer

Darius Rucker, American singer/songwriter

Janet Jackson, American singer

Helena Bonham Carter, British actress

Zola Budd, South African runner

Halle Berry, American actress

Lisa Stansfield, British singer

C. Thomas Howell, American actor

Sinéad O'Connor, Irish singer

Kiefer Sutherland, American actor

Bill Goldberg, American wrestler

Justine Bateman, American actress

Salma Hayek, Mexican actress

Bennie Blades, American football player

Adam Sandler, American actor

John Cusack, American actor

Mary Stuart Masterson, American actress

Mike Tyson, American boxer

Dean Cain, American actor

Billy Mayfair, American golfer

Julianna Margulies, American actress

Jason Patric, American actor

John Daly, American golfer

Samantha Fox, British model and singer

Sophie Marceau, French actress

Adam Horovitz, American rapper

David Schwimmer, American actor

Cindy Crawford, American model

Billy Zane, American actor

Téa Leoni, American actress

Jennifer Grant, American actress

Turn 30 in 2006

Mark Philippoussis, Australian tennis player

J. C. Chasez, American singer

Freddie Prinze Jr., American actor

Reese Witherspoon, American actress

Keri Russell, American actress

Colin Farrell, Irish actor

Virginie Ledoyen, French actress

Jennifer Capriati, American tennis player

Emma Bunton, British singer

Melissa Joan Hart, American actress

Candace Cameron Bure, American actress

Anna Friel, British actress

50 Cent, American rapper

Ronaldo, Brazilian footballer

Ja Rule, American rapper

Lindsay Davenport, American tennis player

Gustavo Kuerten, Brazilian tennis player

Blu Cantrell, American singer

Alicia Silverstone, American actress

Ellen Macarthur, British yachtswoman

Turn 25 in 2006

Elijah Wood, American actor

Justin Timberlake, American singer

Paris Hilton, American socialite

Julia Stiles, American actress

Jessica Alba, American actress

Zara Phillips, British royal

Anna Kournikova, Russian tennis player

Beyoncé Knowles, American singer

Jonathan Taylor Thomas, American actor

Natalie Portman, Israeli-born actress and model

Serena Williams, American tennis player

Britney Spears, American singer

Alicia Keys, American singer

Lleyton Hewitt, Australian tennis player

Bryce Dallas Howard, American actress

Roger Federer, Swiss tennis player

Sienna Miller, British actress

Turn 21 in 2006

Jack Osbourne, Ozzy's son

Keira Knightley, British actress

Michelle Trachtenberg, American actress

Turn 20 in 2006

Charlotte Church, British singer

Jamie Bell, British actor

Mary-Kate and Ashley Olsen, American actresses

Lindsay Lohan, American actress

Born on the Same Day

Barry Goldwater and Dana Andrews (January 1, 1909)

John Paul Jones and Victoria Principal (January 3, 1946)

Julia Ormond, Guy Forget and Beth Gibbons (January 4, 1965)

Robert Duvall and Alfred Brendel (January 5, 1931)

Umberto Eco and Raisa Gorbachev (January 5, 1932)

Capucine and E. L. Doctorow (January 6, 1931)

Nevil Shute and Al Capone (January 17, 1899)

Benny Hill and Telly Savalas (January 21, 1924)

Plácido Domingo and Richie Havens (January 21, 1941)

Randolph Scott and Sergei Eisenstein (January 23, 1898)

Neil Diamond and Aaron Neville (January 24, 1941)

Vanessa Redgrave and Boris Spassky (January 30, 1937)

Sherilyn Fenn, Princess Stephanie of Monaco and Brandon Lee (February 1, 1965)

Farrah Fawcett and Melanie (February 2, 1947)

Charles Lindbergh and Hartley Shawcross (February 4, 1902)

Red Buttons and Andreas Papandreou (February 5, 1919)

Sven Goran Eriksson, Christopher Guest and Barbara Hershey (February 5, 1948)

Rip Torn and Mamie Van Doren (February 6, 1931)

Garth Brooks and Eddie Izzard (February 7, 1962)

Carmen Miranda and Dean Rusk (February 9, 1909)

Jimmy Durante and Bill Tilden (February 10, 1893)

Simon MacCorkindale and Michael McDonald (February 12, 1952)

Alan Parker and Carl Bernstein (February 14, 1944)

Melissa Manchester and Jane Seymour (February 15, 1951)

Jeremy Edwards and Denise Richards (February 17, 1971)

Anthony Head and Patricia Hearst (February 20, 1954)

Kurt Cobain and Andrew Shue (February 20, 1967)

Alan Rickman and Tyne Daly (February 21, 1946)

Jonathan Demme and Tom Okker (February 22, 1944)

Denis Law and Pete Duel (February 24, 1940)

Mario Andretti and Joe South (February 28, 1940)

Mike D'Abo and Roger Daltrey (March 1, 1944)

Catherine Bach and Ron Howard (March 1, 1954)

John Irving and Lou Reed (March 2, 1942)

James Doohan and Ronald Searle (March 3, 1920)

Kenny Dalglish and Chris Rea (March 4, 1951)

Alan Greenspan and Andrzej Wajda (March 6, 1926)

Kiki Dee and Rob Reiner (March 6, 1947)

Trish Van Devere and Bobby Fischer (March 9, 1943)

John B. Sebastian and Patti Boyd (March 17, 1944)

Spike Lee and Theresa Russell (March 20, 1957)

Matthew Broderick and Rosie O'Donnell (March 21, 1962)

Stephen Sondheim and Pat Robertson (March 22, 1930)

Aretha Franklin and Richard O'Brien (March 25, 1942)

Shirley Jones and Richard Chamberlain (March 31, 1934)

Al Gore and Rhea Perlman (March 31, 1948)

Marsha Mason and Wayne Newton (April 3, 1942)

Natasha Lyonne and Heath Ledger (April 4, 1979)

Bette Davis and Herbert von Karajan (April 5, 1908)

Seamus Heaney and Paul Sorvino (April 13, 1939)

Bishop Abel Muzorewa and Rod Steiger (April 14, 1925)

Harold Lloyd and Joan Miró (April 20, 1893)

Richard E. Grant and Peter Howitt (May 5, 1957)

Peter Benchley and Ricky Nelson (May 8, 1940)

Katharine Hepburn and Leslie Charteris (May 12, 1907)

George Lucas and Francesca Annis (May 14, 1944)

Bob Dylan and Harold Melvin (May 24, 1941)

Matt Busby and Aldo Gucci (May 26, 1909)

Hubert Humphrey and Vincent Price (May 27, 1911)

Tara Lipinski and Leelee Sobieski (June 10, 1982)

Carmine Coppola and Jacques Cousteau (June 11, 1910)

Johnny Hallyday and Xaviera Hollander (June 15, 1943)

Paul McCartney and Roger Ebert (June 18, 1942)

Chet Atkins and Audie Murphy (June 20, 1924)

King Edward VIII, Duke of Windsor and Alfred Kinsey (June 23, 1894)

Jamie Farr and Sydney Pollack (July 1, 1934)

Gina Lollobrigida and Neil Simon (July 4, 1927)

Vladimir Ashkenazy, Ned Beatty and Gene Chandler (July 6, 1937)

Louis Jordan and Nelson Rockefeller (July 8, 1908)

Courtney Love and Gianluca Vialli (July 9, 1964)

Harrison Ford and Roger McGuinn (July 13, 1942)

Linda Ronstadt and the Sultan of Brunei (July 15, 1946)

Lolita Davidovich and Forest Whitaker (July 15, 1961)

Donald Sutherland and Diahann Carroll (July 17, 1935)

Phoebe Snow and David Hasselhoff (July 17, 1952)

Albert Brooks and Don Henley (July 22, 1947)

Geraldine Chaplin and Sherry Lansing (July 31, 1944)

James Baldwin and Carroll O'Connor (August 2, 1924)

Joan Hickson and John Huston (August 5, 1906)

Garrison Keillor and B. J. Thomas (August 7, 1942)

Rory Calhoun and Esther Williams (August 8, 1922)

Robert Culp and Tony Trabert (August 16, 1930)

Nelson Piquet and Guillermo Vilas (August 17, 1952)

Johnny Nash and Jill St. John (August 19, 1940)

Kevin Dillon and Kyra Sedgwick (August 19, 1965)

Shelley Long and Rick Springfield (August 23, 1949)

John Savage and Gene Simmons (August 25, 1949)

Blair Underwood and Joanne Whalley (August 25, 1964)

Van Morrison and Itzhak Perlman (August 31, 1945)

Freddie Mercury, Buddy Miles and Loudon Wainwright III (September 5, 1946)

Herbert Lom, Ferdinand Marcos and Jessica Mitford (September 11, 1917)

Jacqueline Bisset and Peter Cetera (September 13, 1944)

Charles Haughey and B. B. King (September 16, 1925)

Scott Baio and Catherine Oxenberg (September 22, 1961)

Mary Beth Hurt and Olivia Newton-John (September 26, 1948)

Denis Lawson and Meat Loaf (September 27, 1947)

Madeline Kahn and Ian McShane (September 29, 1942)

Jimmy Carter and William Rehnquist (October 1, 1924)

Laurence Harvey and George Peppard (October 1, 1928)

Camille Saint-Saëns and Alastair Sim (October 9, 1900)

Sam Moore and Luciano Pavarotti (October 12, 1935)

Lenny Bruce and Margaret Thatcher (October 13, 1925)

Margot Kidder and George Wendt (October 17, 1948)

Chuck Berry and Klaus Kinski (October 18, 1926)

Derek Jacobi and Christopher Lloyd (October 22, 1938)

Jenny McCarthy and Toni Collette (November 1, 1972)

Michael Dukakis and Albert Reynolds (November 3, 1933)

Puff Daddy and Matthew McConaughey (November 4, 1969)

Kazuo Ishiguro and Rickie Lee Jones (November 8, 1954)

Bob Gaudio and Martin Scorsese (November 17, 1942)

Dr. John the Night Tripper and Natalya Makarova (November 21, 1940)

Billy Connolly and Marlin Fitzwater (November 24, 1942)

Jacques Chirac and Diane Ladd (November 29, 1932)

Jaco Pastorius and Treat Williams (December 1, 1951)

John Cassavetes and Bob Hawke (December 9, 1929)

Rita Moreno and Bhagwan Shree Rajneesh (December 11, 1931)

Patty Duke, Michael Ovitz and Stan Smith (December 14, 1946)

Donald Regan and Kurt Waldheim (December 21, 1918)

Pure Trivia, III

The oldest known vegetable is the pea.

To strengthen a Damascus sword, the blade was plunged into a slave.

Catherine the Great relaxed by being tickled.

A coward was originally a boy who took care of cows.

There are 2,598,960 possible hands in a five-card poker game.

Cows can be identified by nose prints.

Eighty-two percent of the workers on the Panama Canal suffered from malaria.

Sixty percent of all U.S. potato products originate in Idaho.

The Forth railway bridge in Scotland is a meter longer in summer than in winter as a result of thermal expansion.

In the Andes, time is often measured by how long it takes to smoke a cigarette.

Brazil got its name from the nut, not the other way around.

It would take about 2 million hydrogen atoms to cover the period at the end of this sentence.

Dirty snow melts more quickly than clean snow.

The model ape used in the 1933 film *King Kong* was 18 inches tall.

Rodin's *The Thinker* is a portrait of the Italian poet Dante.

Johann Sebastian Bach once walked 230 miles to hear the organist at Lübeck in Germany.

After retiring from boxing, ex–world heavyweight champion Gene Tunney lectured on Shakespeare at Yale University.

The Beatles song **"A Day in the Life"** ends with a note sustained for 40 seconds.

Miss Piggy's measurements are 27-20-32.

In 1517, *The Mona Lisa* was bought by King Francis I of France to hang in a bathroom.

Salvador Dalí once arrived at an art exhibition in a limousine filled with turnips.

"Mary, Mary, Quite Contrary" was based on Mary, Queen of Scots.

There are 256 semihemidemisemiquavers in a breve.

There are two independent nations in Europe smaller than New York's Central Park: Vatican City and Monaco.

If the world's total land area were divided equally among the world's people, each person would get 8.5 acres.

Seattle, like Rome, was built on seven hills.

The Dutch town of Leeuwarden can be spelled 225 different ways.

The geographical center of North America is in North Dakota.

The only city whose name can be spelled completely with vowels is Aiea in Hawaii.

John Wilkes Booth's brother once saved the life of Abraham Lincoln's son.

A Guide to 'Strine (Australian Slang)

Bend the elbow (to) = have a drink (as in, "G'day, sport, fancy bending the elbow?")

Bonza or beaut = wonderful, great

Chook = chicken (as eaten on a "barbie")

Crook = unwell (as in "Strewth, I'm crook")

Dead as a dead dingo's donga = in a parlous condition

Drink with the flies (to) = to drink alone (as in, "That cobber's drinking with the flies!")

Dunny = toilet

Fair dinkum = the real thing (sometimes uttered in spite of oneself, as in, "Fair dinkum, that Pom can bat.")

Fair go = good chance (as in, "Shane's got a fair go of taking a wicket against these Pommy bastards.")

Godzone = God's own country (i.e., Australia)

Grog = booze ("BYOG" on an invitation means "bring your own grog")

Hit your kick = open your wallet (as in, "Come on, blue, hit your kick and pay for those tinnies.")

Hooly dooly = I say! (as in, "Hooly dooly, have you seen the state of that dunny?")

Ripper = super

A sausage short of a barbie = **not in possession of all one's** faculties

She'll be right = no problem (as in, "I'll be there at the cricket, she'll be right.")

Spit the dummie = lose one's cool (as in, "I think that bloke's spitting the dummie.")

Spunky = good-looking (as in, "That Kylie sure is spunky.")

True blue = honest or straight (said approvingly, as in, "He may be an ocker, but he's true blue").

Tucker = food

Wowser = killjoy, spoilsport

Words

ALMOST is the longest word in the English language with all the letters in alphabetical order. APPEASES, ARRAIGN-ING, HOTSHOTS, SIGNINGS and TEAMMATE all have letters that occur twice and only twice.

The syllable-OUGH can be pronounced eight different ways—as evidenced by the following sentence: "A rough, dough-faced, thoughtful ploughman emerged

from a slough to walk through the streets of
Scarborough, and coughing."

The sentence "He believed Caesar could see people seizing the seas," contains seven different spellings of the "ee" sound.

In English, only three words have a letter that repeats six times: DEGENERESCENCE (six Es), INDIVISIBILITY (six Is) and NONANNOUNCEMENT (six Ns).

The French equivalent of "The quick brown fox jumps over the lazy dog," a sentence containing every letter of the alphabet (useful when learning to type), is *"Allez porter ce vieux whisky au juge blond qui fume un Havane,"* which translates as "Go and take this old whiskey to the fair-haired judge smoking the Havana cigar."

The word QUIZ was allegedly invented in 1780 by a Dublin theater manager, who bet he could introduce a new word of no meaning into the language within twenty-four hours.

Alice in Wonderland author Lewis Carroll invented the word CHORTLE—a combination of "chuckle" and "snort."

Dr. Seuss invented the word NERD for his 1950 book *If I Ran the Zoo.*

The word QUEUEING is the only English word with five consecutive vowels.

words

WEDLOCK is derived from the old English words for "pledge" (*wed*) and "action" (*lac*).

DIXIE is derived from the French word for "ten"—*dix*—and was first used by a New Orleans bank that issued French-American ten-dollar bills. Later the word expanded to represent the whole of the southern United States.

The shortest English word that contains the letters A, B, C, D, E and F is FEEDBACK.

The word FREELANCE comes from a knight whose lance was free for hire.

The word SHERIFF comes from "shire reeve." In feudal England, each shire had a reeve who upheld the law for that shire.

The Sanskrit word for "war" means "desire for more cows."

SOS doesn't stand for "save our ship" or "save our souls." It was chosen by a 1908 international conference on Morse code because the letters S and O were easy to remember. S is dot-dot-dot, O is dash-dash-dash.

The word CORDUROY comes from the French *cord du roi,* or "cloth of the king."

AFGHANISTAN, KIRGHISTAN and TUVALU are the only countries with three consecutive letters in their names.

RESIGN has two opposed meanings, depending on its pronunciation ("to quit" and "to sign again").

The word SET has the highest number of separate definitions in *The Oxford English Dictionary.*

In Chinese, the words for "crisis" and "opportunity" are the same.

UNDERGROUND and UNDERFUND are the only two words in the English language that begin and end with the letters "und."

The Chinese ideogram for "trouble" shows "two women living under one roof."

Only four words in the English language end in "dous": TREMENDOUS, HORRENDOUS, HAZARDOUS and STUPENDOUS.

The tennis player GORAN IVANISEVIC has the longest name of a celebrity that alternates consonants and vowels.

UNITED ARAB EMIRATES is the longest name of a country consisting of alternating vowels and consonants.

TARAMASALATA (a type of Greek salad) and GALATASARAY (name of a Turkish football club) each have an A for every other letter.

TAXI is spelled the same way in English, French, German, Swedish, Spanish, Danish, Norwegian, Dutch, Czech and Portuguese.

The word THEREIN contains thirteen words spelled with consecutive letters: the, he, her, er, here, I, there, ere, rein, re, in, therein and herein.

SWIMS is the longest word with 180-degree rotational symmetry (if you were to view it upside down, it would still be the same word, and perfectly readable).

UNPROSPEROUSNESS is the longest word in which no letter occurs only once.

The letters www as an abbreviation for "World Wide Web" have nine spoken syllables, whereas the term being abbreviated has only three spoken syllables.

In French, OISEAU (bird) is the shortest word containing all five vowels.

ULTRAREVOLUTIONARIES has each vowel exactly twice.

FACETIOUS and ABSTEMIOUS contain the five vowels in alphabetical order.

SUBCONTINENTAL, UNCOMPLIMENTARY and DUOLITERAL contain the five vowels in reverse alphabetical order.

The shortest sentence in the English language is "Go!"

PLIERS is a word with no singular form. Other such words are ALMS, CATTLE, EAVES and SCISSORS.

ACCEDED, BAGGAGE, CABBAGE, DEFACED, EFFACED and FEEDBAG are seven-letter words that can be played on a musical instrument.

EARTHLING is first found in print in 1593. Other surprisingly old words are SPACESHIP (1894), ACID RAIN (1858),

ANTACID (1753), HAIRDRESSER (1771), MOLE (in connection with espionage, 1622, by Sir Francis Bacon), FUNK (a strong smell, 1623; a state of panic, 1743), MILKY WAY (circa 1384, but earlier in Latin) and MS. (used instead of Miss or Mrs., 1949).

EWE and YOU are pronounced exactly the same, yet share no letters in common.

The words BORSCHTS, LATCHSTRING, CATCHPHRASE, and WELTSCHMERZ each have six consonants in a row.

Tongue Twisters

Six sharp smart sharks.

The sixth sick sheik's sixth sheep's sick.

If Stu chews shoes, should Stu choose the shoes he chews?

Rory the warrior and Roger the worrier were wrongly reared in a rural brewery.

Black-back bat.

Sheena leads, Sheila needs.

Wunwun was a racehorse, Tutu was one, too. Wunwun won one race, Tutu won one, too.

A box of biscuits, a batch of mixed biscuits.

The local yokel yodels.

Eleven benevolent elephants.

Red lorry, yellow lorry, red lorry, yellow lorry.

Is this your sister's sixth zither, sir?

A big black bug bit a big black bear, made the big black bear bleed blood.

Scissors sizzle, thistles sizzle.

Lesser leather never weathered wetter weather better.

We shall surely see the sun shine soon.

A noisy noise annoys an oyster.

Three free throws.

Cheap ship trip.

How much wood would a woodchuck chuck if a woodchuck could chuck wood?

Mrs. Smith's Fish Sauce Shop.

Black bug's blood.

Fred fed Ted bread and Ted fed Fred bread.

Six slick slim sick sycamore saplings.

Irish wristwatch.

Six slippery snails slid slowly seaward.

Friendly Frank flips fine flapjacks.

Selfish shellfish.

Peter Piper picked a peck of pickled peppers.

Did Peter Piper pick a peck of pickled peppers?

If Peter Piper picked a peck of pickled peppers,

Where's the peck of pickled peppers Peter Piper picked?

Botox Treatments

Madonna, Cliff Richard, Patsy Kensit, Joan Rivers, Elizabeth Hurley, Céline Dion, Kirstie Alley, Tom Cruise, Jamie Lee Curtis

Face Lifts

Loni Anderson, Cher, Jane Fonda, Dolly Parton, Joan Rivers, Ivana Trump, Mary Tyler Moore, Angela Lansbury, Roseanne, Liberace, Lucille Ball, Gary Cooper, Joan Crawford, Julie Christie, Marlene Dietrich, Rita Hayworth, Kirk Douglas, Henry Fonda, Michael Jackson, Dean Martin, Jacqueline Kennedy Onassis, Mary Pickford, Elvis Presley, Debbie Reynolds, Frank Sinatra, Barbara Stanwyck, Elizabeth Taylor, Lana Turner, Bea Arthur, Phyllis Diller, Debbie Harry, Barbra Streisand, Sharon Osbourne, Ozzy Osbourne, Julio Iglesias

Had Their Lips Done

Madonna, Cher, Loni Anderson, Pamela Anderson, Melanie Griffith, Ivana Trump, Elizabeth Taylor, Sharon Osbourne

Nose Jobs

Peter O'Toole, Tom Jones, Cher, Marilyn Monroe, Fanny Brice, Barbara Eden, Rhonda Fleming, Annette Funicello, Eva Gabor, Zsa Zsa Gabor, Mitzi Gaynor, Lee Grant, Juliette Greco, Joan Hackett, Carole Landis, Rita Moreno, Stefanie Powers, Jill St. John, Talia Shire, Dinah Shore, Sissy Spacek, Raquel Welch, Milton Berle, Vic Damone, Joel Grey, George Hamilton, Al Jolson, Dean Martin, Lisa Kudrow, Natasha Richardson, Roseanne, Sharon Osbourne, Ozzy Osbourne

Breasts Enlarged

Brigitte Nielsen, Jane Fonda (later had her implants removed), Mariel Hemingway, Melanie Griffith, Iman, Cher, Pamela Anderson, Demi Moore, Dannii Minogue, Gena Lee Nolin, Courtney Love (later had her implants removed), Anna Nicole Smith, Alana Hamilton, Loni Anderson, Heather Locklear, Tanya Roberts, Bo Derek, Jessica Hahn, Donna Rice, Linda Lovelace, Britt Ekland, Paula Abdul, Dyan Cannon, Geena Davis, Jerry Hall, Janet Jackson, LaToya Jackson, Mary Tyler Moore, Jennifer Tilly, Mariah Carey, Mel B (had her implants removed in 2001), Victoria Beckham, Toni Braxton, Carmen Electra

Liposuction

Demi Moore (from her thighs, bottom and stomach)

Joan Rivers (from her thighs)

Anna Nicole Smith (from her stomach)

Melanie Griffith (from her stomach and thighs)

Kenny Rogers (from his stomach)

Roseanne (from her stomach)

Don Johnson (from his chin and cheeks)

Dolly Parton (from her hips and waist)

Alexander McQueen (from his stomach)

Mariah Carey (from her midsection)

Geri Halliwell (from her stomach and thighs)

Jordan (from her thighs)

Jamie Lee Curtis (from underneath her eyes)

Sharon Osbourne (from her neck)

Pierced Nipples

Tim Roth, Tommy Lee, Jaye Davidson, Billy Connolly, Steve Tyler, Liv Tyler, Christina Aguilera, Britney Spears, Janet Jackson

Pierced Tongues

Mel B, Sinéad O'Connor, Janet Jackson

Pierced Navels

Sarah Michelle Gellar, Britney Spears, Serena Williams, Princess Charlotte of Monaco, Madonna, Janet Jackson, Keira Knightley, Zara Phillips

Actors on Acting

"The art of acting is not to act. Once you show them more, what you show them is, in fact, bad acting." (Anthony Hopkins)

"I'm pragmatic. American actors tear themselves apart for a scene. British actors are lazy. We just do it." (Michael Caine)

"It's a difficult business to be in. Bernard Shaw said, 'Never tangle with actresses; they keep such terrible hours'—and he should have known, as he was always trying to tangle with actresses." (Susannah York)

"When an actor marries an actress, they both fight for the mirror." (Burt Reynolds)

"My old drama coach used to say, 'Don't just do something, stand there.'" (Clint Eastwood)

"I didn't say actors are cattle. I said actors should be treated like cattle." (Alfred Hitchcock)

"Being a star is an agent's dream, not an actor's." (Robert Duvall)

"There are lots of reasons why people become actors. Some to hide themselves, and some to show themselves." (Ralph Richardson)

"An actor's a guy who, if you ain't talking about him, he ain't listening." (Marlon Brando)

"Basically, when you whittle everything away, I'm a grown man who puts on makeup." (Brad Pitt)

"I always say that acting isn't conducive to life." (Cindy Crawford)

"Never mistake having a career with having a life." (Sean Young)

"Acting is not an important job. Plumbing is." (Spencer Tracy)

"You gotta be a nut to be in this profession." (Rod Steiger)

"It does seem sometimes that acting is hardly the occupation of an adult." (Laurence Olivier)

"Actors are rogues and vagabonds. Or they ought to be." (Helen Mirren)

"Nobody became an actor because he had a good childhood." (William H. Macy)

"Don't think for a moment that I'm really like any of the characters I've played. I'm not—that's why it's called acting." (Leonardo DiCaprio)

Mnemonics and Memory Aids

The kings and queens of England and the United Kingdom since 1066:

Willie, Willie, Harry, Ste
Harry, Dick, John, Harry three
One two three Edward, Richard two,
Henry four, five, six, then who?
Edward four, five, Dick the bad,
Harry twain, then Ned the lad,
Mary, Bessie, James the vain,
Charlie, Charlie, James again,
William and Mary, Ann Gloria
Four Georges, William, then Victoria,
Edward, George, then Ned the eighth
Quickly goes and abdicateth,
Leaving George, then Liz the second,
And with Charlie next it's reckoned
That's the way our monarchs lie
Since Harold got it in the eye!

The order of planets in distance from the Sun— Mercury, Venus, Earth, Mars, Jupiter, Saturn, Uranus, Neptune, Pluto—My Very Easy Method: Just Set Up Nine Planets.

The order of colors in the rainbow—red, orange, yellow, green, blue, indigo, violet—Richard Of York Gave Battle In Vain.

The order of geological time periods—Cambrian, Ordovician, Silurian, Devonian, Carboniferous, Permian, Triassic, Jurassic, Cretaceous, Paleocene, Eocene, Oligocene, Miocene, Pliocene, Pleistocene, Recent—Cows Often Sit Down Carefully. Perhaps Their Joints Creak? Persistent Early Oiling Might Prevent Painful Rheumatism.

The countries of Central America in geographical order—Belize, Guatemala, Honduras, Nicaragua, Costa Rica, Panama—BeeGee's Hen! Se 'er Pee?

The order of Mohs hardness scale, from 1 to 10—talc, gypsum, calcite, fluorite, apatite, orthoclase feldspar, quartz, topaz, corundum, diamond—Toronto Girls Can Flirt, And Other Queer Things Can Do.

The order of sharps in music—FCGDAEB—Father Charles Goes Down And Ends Battle.

The order of notes to which guitar strings should be tuned—EBGDAE—Easter Bunnies Get Drunk At Easter.

The order of notes represented by the lines on the treble clef stave—EGBDF—Every Good Boy Does Fine.

The order of taxonomy in biology—kingdom, phylum, class, order, family, genus, species—Kids Prefer Cheese Over Fried Green Spinach.

The four oceans—Indian, Arctic, Atlantic, Pacific—I Am A Person.

The seven continents—Europe, Antarctica, Asia, Africa, Australia, North America, South America—Eat AN ASpirin AFter AUgmenting Noah's Ship.

The Great Lakes—Huron, Ontario, Michigan, Erie, Superior—HOMES. For the Great Lakes in order of size—Superior, Huron, Michigan, Erie, Ontario—Sam's Horse Must Eat Oats.

The Confederate States of America—South Carolina, Louisiana, Georgia, North Carolina, Alabama, Arkansas, Virginia, Mississippi, Florida, Tennessee and Texas—Sultry Carol Languished Grumpily Near Carl, Always Aware Virginal Men Frequently Take Time.

2001: A Space Oddity: Apes, Bones, Cosmic Device . . . Evolution! Floating Giant Hub. Investigate Jupiter. Komputer Loopy. Man Nears Outsized Plinth. Queer Readings. Starry Turbulence. Unexpected Very Weird Xyschedelia Yielding Zen.

Lucky Charms

Billy Crystal: a toothbrush he used to pretend was a microphone when he was a child. He now carries it onstage whenever he performs.

Luciano Pavarotti: a bent nail, which he always wears in his top pocket when he performs.

Damon Hill: has an Austrian lucky charm called a *Gamsbart.* It's a tassel made of goat hair and was given to Hill by his trainer, Erwine Gollner.

Yves Saint Laurent: a jewel, a heart made of gray diamonds with rubies. "It's at home, in a secret place. I only take it out for collections."

Dustin Hoffman, Phil Collins, Johnny Mathis, Liza Minnelli, Steven Spielberg, Cate Blanchett, Britney Spears (after hypnosis failed, she painted her nails with a red-hot pepper polish that burned her tongue), Mel B (toenails), Elijah Wood, Bryan Ferry

Chain-Smokers

Donatella Versace, Joaquin Phoenix, F. W. de Klerk, Gérard Depardieu, Tom Clancy, Robbie Williams, Kate Moss, Michel Platini

Recovering Alcoholics

Mel Gibson, Barry Humphries, Anthony Hopkins, Eric Clapton, Dick Van Dyke, Buzz Aldrin, Patrick Swayze, John Daly, Roseanne, Dennis Quaid, Drew Barrymore, Ken Kercheval, Elizabeth Taylor, Ringo Starr, Sharon Gless, Elton John, Gary Oldman, Robbie Williams, Anne Robinson

Had/Have an Alcoholic Parent

Marlon Brando (both)

Jonathan Winters (father)

Suzanne Somers (father)

Lauren Hutton (mother)

Alec Guinness (mother)

Charles Chaplin (father)

Adam Ant (father)

Demi Moore (mother)

Richard Burton (father)

Meat Loaf (father)

Eminem (mother)

Sinéad O'Connor (mother)

Ben Affleck (father)

Nora Ephron (both)

Halle Berry (father)

Rod Steiger (mother)

Rosemary Clooney
(both)

Brian Wilson (mother)

Gérard Depardieu (father)

Andie MacDowell (mother)

Samantha Mumba (father)

Tom Cruise (father)

Ronald Reagan (father)

Malcolm McDowell (father)

Money

American Airlines saved $40,000 in 1987 by eliminating one olive from each salad served in first class.

More Monopoly money is printed in a year than real money throughout the world.

Lee Harvey Oswald's cadaver tag sold at auction for $6,600 in 1992.

In 1979, Judy Garland's false eyelashes were sold at auction for $125.

During World War II, W. C. Fields kept $50,000 in Germany "in case the little bastard wins."

Sigmund Freud bought his first sample of cocaine for $1.27 per gram.

Woodpecker scalps, porpoise teeth and giraffe tails have all been used as money.

There are two credit cards for every person in the United States.

In Monopoly, the most money you can lose in one trip around the board (going to jail only once) is $26,040. The most money you can lose in one turn is $5,070. If, on the other hand, no one ever buys anything, players could eventually break the bank.

Ninety-seven percent of paper money in the United States contains traces of cocaine.

After the Civil War, the United States sued Great Britain for damages caused by ships the British had built for the Confederacy. The United States asked for $1 billion but settled for $25 million.

Went Bankrupt

Margot Kidder, Walt Disney, Eddie Fisher, Grace Jones, Mark Twain, Mickey Rooney, MC Hammer, Frank Lloyd Wright, Toni Braxton

Polonius's Advice to His Son, Laertes, in *Hamlet*

Yet here, Laertes! Aboard, aboard for shame!
The wind sits in the shoulder of your sail,
And you are stay'd for.
There . . . my blessing with thee!
And these few precepts in thy memory
Look thou character. Give thy thoughts no tongue,
Nor any unproportion'd thought his act.
Be thou familiar, but by no means vulgar.
Those friends thou hast, and their adoption tried,
Grapple them to thy soul with hoops of steel;
But do not dull thy palm with entertainment
Of each new-hatch'd, unfledg'd comrade. Beware
Of entrance to a quarrel but, being in,
Bear't that th' opposed may beware of thee.
Give every man thy ear, but few thy voice;
Take each man's censure, but reserve thy judgement.
Costly thy habit as thy purse can buy,
But not express'd in fancy; rich,
    not gaudy;
For the apparel oft proclaims the
    man;
And they in France of the
    best rank and station
Are of a most select and
    generous chief in that.
Neither a borrower, nor a
    lender be;

For loan oft loses both itself and friend,
And borrowing dulls the edge of husbandry.
This above all: to thine own self be true,
And it must follow, as the night the day,
Thou canst not then be false to any man.
Farewell: my blessing season this in thee!

Anagrams

ORDER IN YAWN—Winona Ryder

SO CHECK JAIL, MAN—Michael Jackson

SCREEN ANNOY—Sean Connery

BIG LEMONS—Mel Gibson

BRAIN CREEPS ON—Pierce Brosnan

RISK BIG NAME?—Kim Basinger

I LIKE 'EM YOUNG—Kylie Minogue

"CREEP," SHE'LL MOAN—Elle Macpherson

ANIMAL WHISTLER—William Shatner

ONLY I CAN THRILL—Hillary Clinton

DEAR DEAR, RUDE PIG—Gérard Depardieu

ME MOODIER—Demi Moore

LIBRARY WOMAN—Barry Manilow

CLOSE EVIL SLOT—Elvis Costello

STORY BLUNDER—Burt Reynolds

GOT SO WEIRD—Tiger Woods

A WILD OLD MENACE—Andie MacDowell

HEADING LOW—Goldie Hawn

LIKES REALITY—Kirstie Alley

LENT WORTHY GAWP—Gwyneth Paltrow

NO, I AM CRAZED—Cameron Diaz

TAKES CLEAN BIKE—Kate Beckinsale

GEOLOGY ENCORE—George Clooney

SLICK OR FATAL CHAT—Calista Flockhart

MERRY GLEE MASK—Kelsey Grammer

BURY HARSHER IMP—Barry Humphries

TALKING ON SEX—Alex Kingston

I DO RAW SULK—Lisa Kudrow

SAME JOURNEY—Jane Seymour

ADORING SLAVES—Gavin Rossdale

TURNED STINKS—Kirsten Dunst

MEET JUBILANT RISK—Justin Timberlake

JEER TO LAD—Jared Leto

I'M A TRUE BOGEY—Tobey Maguire

ADJOINING FLAMES—James Gandolfini

CRASH MUCH EACH MILE—Michael Schumacher

EMPHATIC LIES—Michael Stipe

I'M MORALS NANNY—Marilyn Manson

CIAO GLANCES—Nicolas Cage

WE AVOID BID—David Bowie

WOMANLY TIES—Emily Watson

NEVER NOT SICK—Kevin Costner

ODD BAT FRINGE—Bridget Fonda

SO RELAX—Axl Rose

HER SLOW CRY—Sheryl Crow

CRITICS IN CHAIR—Christina Ricci

A NAME VIRUS—Mena Suvari

OUR SNEERS—Rene Russo

HAIRS DISCERNED—Denise Richards

ANIMAL CRANK—Alan Rickman

IN CLEAN CLOTHES—Chelsea Clinton

EASY RISING—Gary Sinise

HOME TWIT NAMED—Matthew Modine

AS SPEAKER JARS CHAIR—Sarah Jessica Parker

WATERY BANTER—Warren Beatty

INDOOR DANCER—Donna D'Errico

GROW ACNE GERM—Ewan McGregor

NAKED SHOUT—Kate Hudson

CANCEL THAT BET—Cate Blanchett

BENIGN NEAT TEN—Annette Bening

JAIL GENIAL ONE—Angelina Jolie

IN MOCK DENIAL—Nicole Kidman

COY VOLUNTEER—Courtney Love

CAN RESEARCH ARMPIT—Charisma Carpenter

ENVY SICK APE—Kevin Spacey

CONK ALL ABSURD—Sandra Bullock

HARASSED NEAT THING—Natasha Henstridge

THIS INERT RASCAL—Christian Slater

DON'T REAR DOWN—Edward Norton

RARE MYTH WEPT—Matthew Perry

STERN LIBEL—Ben Stiller

THEATER RICH—Teri Hatcher

REPLENISH FAN—Ralph Fiennes

TRICK IN ARMY—Ricky Martin

I'M A TORSO—Tori Amos

GLIB REPARTEE—Peter Gabriel

I AM RACY, HEAR?—Mariah Carey

MOLEST ME—ENJOY!—Tommy Lee Jones

I'M STAR EVENT—Steve Martin

ONE POSH LIAR—Sophia Loren

RICH RED RAGE—Richard Gere

HE'S MAGICAL, LOUD—Michael Douglas

METAL OAF—Meat Loaf

FRIENDLY JEERS—Jerry Seinfeld

NO BRAINS ON A DATE—Antonio Banderas

WET SINK TALE—Kate Winslet

FINDS A HORROR—Harrison Ford

GRIN BY A REBEL—Gabriel Byrne

A SEVERE NUKE—Keanu Reeves

IDEAL SINEWY LAD—Daniel Day-Lewis

I AM ONLY A LASS—Alyssa Milano

Remarkable People

Tommy Lee has a Starbucks in his house.

Kim Basinger puts sour cream and lemon juice in her bathwater.

Marlon Brando's occupation on his passport was "Shepherd."

Julio Iglesias once had five gallons of water flown from Miami to L.A. so he could wash his hair.

Anthony Hopkins used to be able to hypnotize people by pulling their earlobes.

David Lynch always leaves one shoelace untied.

Michael Jackson owns the rights to the South Carolina state anthem.

Debra Winger was the voice of ET.

Woody Allen won't take a shower if the drain is in the middle.

Queen Latifah wears the key for the motorcycle on which her brother suffered a fatal crash on a chain around her neck.

John Grisham shaves just once a week—before church on Sunday.

Jewel is a champion yodeler—and has been since her childhood (even though it is "impossible" for children to yodel because their vocal cords aren't sufficiently developed).

Robert Downey Jr. once spent a night in jail with Tommy Lee.

Cate Blanchett gave her husband plaster casts of her ears as a present.

Arm wrestling is one of Helena Bonham Carter's favorite pastimes.

Renée Zellweger keeps a "grateful journal," a collection of her favorite things, on her bedside table.

Cindy Crawford believes placentas should be buried under trees for good luck.

P. Diddy wears a diamond-encrusted watch to protect against pollution from his mobile phone.

As a teenager, Naomi Campbell used to hang around waiting for an autograph outside Boy George's house.

Nicolas Cage was twenty-eight before he first went abroad (to a screening in Cannes). He employs his own pizza chef and has a special pizza oven in his house.

During their marriage, Angelina Jolie and Billy Bob Thornton bought an electric chair for their dining room.

Gisele Bundchen owns over two hundred belts.

James Woods is ambidextrous.

Missy Elliott spends four hours a day on her hair.

Diane Keaton's old college named a street after her in 2000.

Shaggy was a U.S. Marine and served in the first Gulf War.

 Harrison Ford has a species of spider named after him.

Pure Trivia, IV

Monaco's national orchestra is bigger than its army.

Each episode of *Dr. Kildare* had three suffering patients.

As a young and struggling artist, Pablo Picasso kept warm by burning his own paintings.

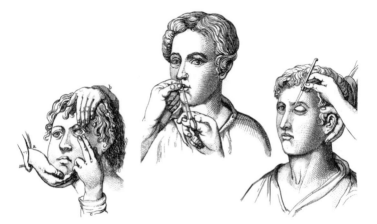

Rin Tin Tin is buried in Père-Lachaise cemetery in Paris.

Enid Blyton, writer of the *Famous Five*, had 59 stories published in 1959.

Pablo Picasso was abandoned by the midwife just after his birth because she thought he was stillborn. He was saved by an uncle.

Ludwig van Beethoven was once arrested for vagrancy.

Dante died on the day he completed his masterpiece, *The Divine Comedy*.

At the height of his addiction, the poet Samuel Taylor Coleridge drank about 2 liters of laudanum (tincture of opium) each week.

Actress Sarah Bernhardt played the part of Juliet (13 years old) when she was 70.

A kilo of lemons contains more sugar than a kilo of strawberries.

About 70 percent of all living organisms in the world are bacteria.

The yo-yo originated in the Philippines, where it was used as a weapon in hunting.

The board game Monopoly was originally rejected by Parker Brothers, who claimed it had 52 fundamental errors.

The screwdriver was invented before the screw.

The screwdriver cocktail was invented by oilmen, who used the tool to stir the drink.

Soda water does not contain soda.

The meter was originally defined as one 10-millionth of the distance from the equator to the pole.

A fully loaded **supertanker** traveling at normal speed takes at least 20 minutes to stop.

North American Indians ate watercress to dissolve stones in the bladder.

In Russia, suppositories cut from fresh potatoes were used for relief from hemorrhoids.

Opium was used widely as a painkiller during the American Civil War. More than a hundred thousand soldiers became addicts.

The females of the Tiwi tribe in the South Pacific are married at birth.

Ralph and Carolyn Cummins had 5 children between 1952 and 1966, all of whom were born on February 20.

The Zambian authorities don't allow tourists to take pictures of Pygmies.

Alexander Graham Bell, inventor of the telephone, never phoned his wife or mother, as both were deaf.

The warrior tribes of Ethiopia used to hang the testicles of those they killed in battle on the ends of their spears.

Eau de cologne was originally marketed as a way of protecting yourself against the plague.

South American gauchos put raw steak under their saddles before starting a day's riding, to tenderize the meat.

There are 240 white dots in a Pac-Man arcade game.

Blackbird, chief of the Omaha Indians, was buried sitting on his favorite horse.

A group of geese on the ground is a gaggle; a group of geese in the air is a skein.

Aeschylus, the founder of classical Greek tragedy, is said to have died when an eagle passing above dropped a tortoise on his head.

After Custer's last stand, Sioux leader Chief Sitting Bull became an entertainer and toured the country with Buffalo Bill's Wild West Show.

Aztec emperor Montezuma had a nephew, Cuitlahac, whose name meant "plenty of excrement."

Bananas contain about 75 percent water.

Chewing gum while peeling onions will keep you from crying.

Chewing gum has rubber as an ingredient.

Coca-Cola was originally green.

Cuckoo clocks come from the Black Forest in Germany—not Switzerland.

An inch of snow falling evenly on an acre of ground is equivalent to about 2,715 gallons of water.

During the Middle Ages, people used spiderwebs to try to cure warts.

In 1967, the American Association of Typographers made a new punctuation mark that was a combination of the question mark and an exclamation point and called it an "interrobang." It was rarely used and hasn't been seen since.

Genghis Khan's cavalry rode female horses so soldiers could drink their milk.

Given sufficient amounts of chocolate as a reward, pigs can master video game skills.

Photographic Memories

Truman Capote,
Simon Wiesenthal,
Robert Mitchum,
Wolfgang Mozart,
Mr. T, Chico Marx

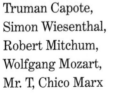

Hotel Suites Named After Them

Arthur C. Clarke (Hotel Club Oceanic, Sri Lanka)

James Galway (Tara Hotel, London)

Barbara Cartland (Heritage Hotel at Helmsdale in Sutherland)

James Michener (Oriental Hotel in Thailand)

Dave Brubeck (Hotel Viking, Newport, Rhode Island)

Samuel Clemens (aka Mark Twain: Painted Lady Hotel, Elmira, New York)

Jenny Lind (Willard Intercontinental, Washington)

Roger Moore (Grand Lido Sans Souci Resort, Ocho Rios, Jamaica)

Agatha Christie (Old Cataract Hotel, Aswan, Egypt)

Marlene Dietrich (Hotel Lancaster, Paris)

Luciano Pavarotti (Pangkor Laut Island Resort, Malaysia)

Michael Jordan (Atlantis Hotel, Bahamas)

Mata Hari (American Hotel, Amsterdam)

John Lennon (Queen Elizabeth Hotel, Montreal)

Liam Neeson (Fitzpatrick Hotel, Chicago)

Marilyn Monroe (Legend Hotel, Kuala Lumpur)

Graham Greene (Sofitel Metropole, Hanoi)

Celebrities and the Number of Pairs of Sneakers They Own

Goldie (1,600)

Mel C (over 200)

Justin Timberlake (450—including every model of Air Jordans ever made)

Johnny Vegas (30)

Craig David (200)

Damon Dash (3,000)

N.B.: P. Diddy throws his away after wearing them for just one day

"Saw" Ghosts

Queen Elizabeth II—When they were children, the queen and her sister, Princess Margaret, believed they saw the ghost of Queen Elizabeth I at Windsor Castle.

Daniel Day-Lewis—He thought he had seen the ghost of his father (the late Poet Laureate Cecil Day-Lewis) when he was acting in *Hamlet* in 1989. When the actor playing the ghost of Hamlet's father said, "I am thy father's spirit," Daniel Day-Lewis went offstage and wouldn't come back—convinced that he'd "seen" his father.

Sting—He awoke to find a "figure" dressed in Victorian clothes in his room. He thought it was his wife until he saw her in bed next to him. She also saw the apparition, and they held each other tight, staring at it until it faded away, never to return.

Bob Hoskins—Before finding fame, he was working as a porter in Covent Garden and was in a cellar when he "saw" a nun. She held her hands out to him and spoke, but he didn't understand what she said. Later he was told that Covent Garden had formerly been Convent Garden and had been owned by the Benedictines. The legend was that anyone who saw a nun's ghost would have a lucky life.

Prince Charles—Some years ago he and his valet, Ken Stronach, were going into the library at Sandringham when they felt inexplicably cold and became convinced that someone was standing behind them. When they looked around, no one was there. They ran out.

Noah Wyle—His California ranch, bought from Bo Derek, was apparently haunted by the late John Derek. He said that John's ghost kept making "strange noises" when he and his fiancée tried to sleep in the master bedroom, so they moved to a guest bedroom and had the main suite remodeled.

Britney Spears—She says a ghost used to tweak her nipple ring and hide her belongings as she got ready to go out in the mornings.

Joanna Lumley—She was "told" to "leave this place" by an ancient moving man when she moved into the parsonage in Goodnestone, Kent.

N.B.: Ghosts appear in four of Shakespeare's plays: *Julius Caesar, Richard III, Hamlet* and *Macbeth.*

Made It to 100 Years Old

George Burns, Hal Roach, Rose Kennedy, Irving Berlin, Adolph Zukor, Bob Hope, Grandma Moses, Mother Jones, George Abbott, Estelle Winwood, Leni Riefenstahl, Strom Thurmond, Alf Landon

Featured on Stamps

Michael Jackson (Tanzania)

Elton John (Grenada and Australia)

Mick Jagger (St. Vincent)

Whitney Houston (Tanzania)

Cher (Grenada)

Elle Macpherson (Australia)

Arnold Schwarzenegger (Mali)

Dolly Parton (Grenada)

Frank Sinatra (St. Vincent)

Jimmy Connors (Lesotho)

Carl Lewis (Niger)

Eddie Murphy (Tanzania)

Muhammad Ali (Liberia)

Margaret Thatcher (Kenya)

Nick Faldo (St. Vincent)

Stevie Wonder (Tanzania)

Gladys Knight (Tanzania)

Bruce Springsteen (Grenada)

Barbra Streisand (St. Vincent)

George Michael (St. Vincent)

Robert De Niro (Gambia)

Boris Becker (Central African Republic)

Prince (St. Vincent)

Tina Turner (Tanzania)

Björn Borg (Ivory Coast)

Paul Newman (The Maldives)

Elliott Gould (Gambia)

Pelé (Brazil)

John McEnroe (Sierra Leone)

Martina Navratilova (Ivory Coast)

Kirk Douglas (Mali)

The Bee Gees (Isle of Man)

Made Parachute Jumps

Prince Charles, Matt LeBlanc, Billy Connolly, David Hasselhoff

Can Communicate in Sign Language

Jane Fonda, Holly Hunter, William Hurt, Hugh Grant, Sinéad O'Connor, Richard Dreyfuss, Louise Fletcher

Learned to Swim as Adults

Paul McCartney, Tina Turner, Pablo Picasso, Donna D'Errico, Robin Williams

Proficient Magicians

Prince Charles, Muhammad Ali, Norman Schwarzkopf, Michael Jackson, Thomas Levet

Wrote Children's Books

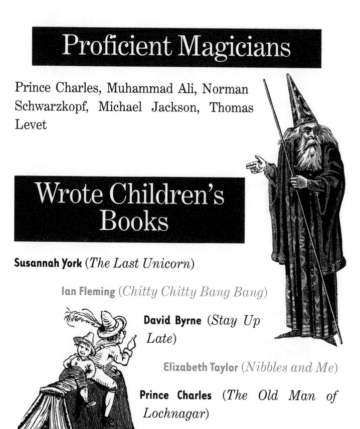

Susannah York (*The Last Unicorn*)

Ian Fleming (*Chitty Chitty Bang Bang*)

David Byrne (*Stay Up Late*)

Elizabeth Taylor (*Nibbles and Me*)

Prince Charles (*The Old Man of Lochnagar*)

Terry Jones (*Lady Cottington's Pressed Fairy Book*)

Colonel Muammar Gaddafi (*The Village, the Village, the Earth, the Earth . . . and the Suicide of the Spaceman*)

      Jamie Lee Curtis (*Where Do Balloons Go?*)

Inventors

Jamie Lee Curtis ("baby wipe diaper")

      Hedy Lamarr (a machine that helped the Americans target U-boats)

Julie Newmar (bottom-shaping tights and a bosom-firming bra)

      Steve McQueen (low-slung bucket seat for racing cars)

Neil Young (portable exercise device)

      Harry Connick Jr. (computer program that allows musicians to follow the score on a screen)

Daryl Hannah (board game entitled "Love It or Hate It")

Had Their Paintings Exhibited

Tony Curtis, David Hemmings, Joni Mitchell, Prince Charles, Anthony Quinn, Bryan Ferry, Ronnie Wood, Sylvester Stallone, Miles Davis, Noël Coward, Adolf Hitler, Paul McCartney, Jeff Bridges, David Bowie, Rod Stewart, Jennifer Aniston (at the Metropolitan Museum of Art in New York), Marilyn Manson, Dennis Hopper, Steve Kanaly, Artie Shaw, Elke Sommer, Red Skelton, Herve Villechaize, Donna Summer, Nelson Mandela

Names of Things You Didn't Know Had Names

The holes in Swiss cheese are called "eyes."

"Mucophagy" is the medical term for "snot-eating," the consumption of the nasal mucus obtained from nose-picking.

The technical term for snapping your fingers is a "fillip."

A poem written to celebrate a wedding is called an "epithalamium."

149

A **"vamp"** is the upper front part of a shoe.

The **"you are here" arrow** on a map is called the "IDEO locator."

The S-shaped opening in a violin is called the "f-hole."

The **little bumps** on the surface of a table-tennis paddle are called "pips."

The infinity symbol is a "lemniscate."

A **holder for a cup or a mug** without handles is called a "zarf."

The word for a gap between your teeth is "diastema."

The **plastic covering** on the end of a shoelace is an "aglet."

Food that's spit out is "chanking."

The **dot above the letter** *i* is called a "tittle."

The metal hoop a lampshade sits on is called a "harp."

The **white tip of the finger and toenail** is called a "lunula," because the end of the nail is rounded like the moon.

A puff of smoke, such as that produced when someone smokes a pipe, is called a "lunt."

A **band worn around the arm** is called a "brassard."

The thin line of cloud that forms behind an aircraft at high altitudes is called a "contrail."

The little finger or toe is called the "minimus."

The symbol produced by the "pound" key (#) is called an "octothorpe."

Illegible handwriting is known as "griffonage."

The word for empty space between the bottle top and the liquid is called "ullage."

"Walla" is a sound engineer's term for room noise.

The act of stretching and yawning is "pandiculation."

One-hundredth of a second is called a "jiffy."

A pig's snout is called a "gruntle."

A "dzo" is the offspring of a yak and a cow.

A cat's whiskers are called "vibrissae."

A "geep" is the offspring of a sheep and a goat.

The little hole in the sink that lets water drain out instead of flowing over the side is called a "porcelator."

The ball on top of a flagpole is called the "truck."

The little lump of flesh just in front of the ear canal is called a "tragus."

The cap on the fire hydrant is called a "bonnet."

N.B.: There is no single word for the back of the knee.

Insurance: A Cautionary Tale

A lawyer from Charlotte, North Carolina, bought a box of very expensive cigars, then insured them against fire. Within a month, having smoked every single one of them—and despite the fact that he hadn't yet paid his first premium—the lawyer filed a claim, declaring that the cigars had been lost "in a series of small fires." The insurance company refused to pay, for the obvious reason: the man had merely consumed the cigars correctly. Nevertheless, the lawyer won.

In handing out his ruling, the judge agreed with the insurance company that the claim was frivolous but stated that the lawyer held a policy from the company in which it had warranted that the cigars were insurable and also guaranteed that it would insure them against fire. It had not defined what was considered to be unacceptable fire and therefore was obliged to pay the claim. The insurance company paid $15,000 to the lawyer for the loss of his cigars in the "fires."

After the lawyer cashed the check, however, the insurance company had him arrested on twenty-four counts of arson. With his own insurance claim used against him, the lawyer was convicted of intentionally burning his insured property and sentenced to twenty-four months in jail and a $24,000 fine.

This is a true story.

Genuine Things Written by Drivers on Insurance Forms

"I didn't think the speed limit applied after midnight."

"**I knew the dog was possessive** about the car, but I would not have asked her to drive it if I had thought there was any risk."

"I consider that neither car was to blame, but if either one was to blame, it would be the other one."

"**I knocked over a man.** He admitted it was his fault, as he had been run over before."

"Coming home, I drove into the wrong house and collided with a tree I don't have."

"**The other car collided** with mine without giving warning of its intentions."

"I collided with a stationary truck coming the other way."

"**In my attempt to kill a fly**, I drove into a telephone pole."

"**I had been shopping for plants all day** and was on my way home. As I reached an intersection, a hedge sprang up, obscuring my vision, and I did not see the other car."

"**I had been driving for forty years** when I fell asleep at the wheel and had an accident."

"**I was on my way to the doctor** with rear-end trouble when my universal joint gave way, causing me to have an accident."

"**My car was legally parked** as it backed into the other vehicle."

"**As I approached the intersection,** a sign suddenly appeared in a place where no sign had ever appeared before, making me unable to avoid the accident."

"**I told the police** I was not injured, but upon removing my hair, I found that I had a fractured skull."

"**I was sure the old fellow** would never make it to the other side of the road when I struck him."

"**I saw a slow-moving,** sad-faced old gentleman as he bounced off the roof of my car."

"**The indirect cause of the accident** was a little guy in a small car with a big mouth."

"**I was thrown from my car** as it left the road and was later found in a ditch by some stray cows."

"**A pedestrian hit me** and went under my car."

"**I thought my window was down,** but I found out it was up when I put my head through it."

"**To avoid hitting** the bumper of the car in front, I struck the pedestrian."

"**The guy was all over the road.** I had to swerve a number of times before I hit him."

"**The pedestrian had no idea** which way to run, so I ran over him."

"**An invisible car** came out of nowhere, struck my car and vanished."

"**A truck backed through** my windshield into my wife's face."

"**I pulled away from the side of the road,** glanced at my mother-in-law and headed over the embankment."

"**The accident happened** because I had one eye on the truck in front, one eye on the pedestrian and the other on the car behind."

"**I started to slow down,** but the traffic was more stationary than I thought."

"**I pulled in to a rest area** with smoke coming from under the hood. I realized the car was on fire, so took my dog and smothered it with a blanket."

Question: "Could either driver have done anything to avoid the accident?" Answer: "Traveled by bus?"

The claimant had collided with a cow. Question: "What warning was given by you?" Answer: "Horn." Question: "What warning was given by the other party?" Answer: "Moo."

"**On approach to the traffic lights,** the car in front suddenly broke."

"**I was going at about seventy or eighty miles per hour** when my girlfriend reached around and grabbed my testicles, so I lost control."

"Windshield broken. Cause unknown. Probably Voodoo."

"**The car in front** hit the pedestrian, but he got up, so I hit him again."

"The telephone pole was approaching. I was attempting to swerve out of the way when I struck the front end."

"**The gentleman behind me** struck me on the backside. He then went to rest in a bush with just his rear end showing."

"I had been learning to drive with power steering. I turned the wheel to what I thought was enough and found myself in a different direction going the opposite way."

"**I was backing my car** out of the driveway in the usual manner when it was struck by the other car in the same place it had been struck several times before."

"When I saw I could not avoid a collision, I stepped on the gas and crashed into the other car."

"**The accident happened** when the right front door of a car came around the corner without giving a signal."

"No one was to blame for the accident, but it would never have happened if the other driver had been alert."

"**I was unable to stop in time,** and my car crashed into the other vehicle. The driver and passengers then left immediately for a vacation with injuries."

"The pedestrian ran for the pavement, but I got him."

"**I saw her look at me twice.** She appeared to be making slow progress when we met on impact."

"The accident occurred when I was attempting to bring my car out of a skid by steering it into the other vehicle."

"The accident was due to another man narrowly missing me."

"The car occupants were stalking deer on the hillside."

"The water in my radiator accidentally froze at midnight."

"I had to turn the car sharper than was necessary, owing to an invisible truck."

"The other man changed his mind, so I had to run into him."

"There was no damage to the car, as the gatepost will testify."

"A dog on the road braked, causing a skid."

"I told the other idiot what he was and went on."

"I can give no details of the accident, as I was concussed at the time."

"Willful damage was done to the upholstery by rats."

"I blew my horn, but it would not work, as it had been stolen."

"I unfortunately ran over a pedestrian, and the old gentleman was taken to hospital much regretting the circumstances."

"Cow wandered into my car. I was afterward informed that the cow was half-witted."

"A bull was standing near, and the fly must have tickled him, as he gored my car."

"If the other driver had stopped a few yards behind himself, the accident would not have happened."

"She suddenly saw me, lost her head, and we met."

"I bumped a lamppost, which was obscured by pedestrians."

"I ran into a shop window and sustained injuries to my wife."

"I misjudged a lady crossing the street."

"Three women were talking to each other, and when two stepped back and one stepped forward, I had to have an accident."

"A lamppost bumped the car, damaging it in two places."

"I left my car unattended for a minute, and, whether by accident or design, it ran away."

Allegedly Genuine Responses Given by Mothers Seeking British Child Support, in the Section Asking for Father's Details

"Regarding the identity of the father of my twins, child A was fathered by [name given]. I am unsure as to the identity of the father of child B, but I believe that he was conceived on the same night."

"I am unsure as to the identity of the father of my child, as I was being sick out of a window when taken unexpectedly from behind. I can provide you with a list of names of men that I think were at the party if this helps."

"I do not know the name of the father of my little girl. She was conceived at a party at [address given], where I had unprotected sex with a man I met that night. I do remember that the sex was so good that I fainted. If you do manage to track down the father, can you send me his phone number? Thanks."

"I don't know the identity of the father of my daughter. He drives a BMW that now has a hole made by my stiletto in one of the door panels. Perhaps you can contact BMW service stations in this area and see if he's had it replaced?"

"I have never had sex with a man. I am awaiting a letter from the pope confirming that my son's conception was immaculate and that he is Christ risen again."

"I cannot tell you the name of child A's dad, as he informs me that to do so would blow his cover and that would have cataclysmic implications for the British economy. I am torn between doing right by you and right by the country. Please advise."

"[Name given] is the father of child A. If you do catch up with him, can you ask him what he did with my AC/DC CDs?"

"From the dates, it seems that my daughter was conceived at EuroDisney. Maybe it really is the Magic Kingdom."

"So much about that night is a blur. The only thing that I remember for sure is Delia Smith did a program about

eggs earlier in the evening. If I'd have stayed in and watched more TV rather than going to the party at [address given], mine might have remained unfertilized."

"I am unsure as to the identity of the father of my baby. After all, when you eat a can of beans, you can't be sure which one made you fart."

Relative Values

Whoopi Goldberg's first grandchild was born on her thirty-fifth birthday.

Hilary Swank is Rob Lowe's sister-in-law.

Zubin Mehta's first ex-wife is married to his brother.

Alicia Silverstone filed for emancipation from her parents at the age of fifteen so that she could work as an adult.

Kathleen Turner and Donna Karan are sisters-in-law.

Use Their Mother's Maiden Name

Shirley MacLaine (Beaty)

Marilyn Monroe (Baker)

Lauren Bacall (Perske)

Shelley Winters (actually, her mother's maiden name was Winter)

Catherine Deneuve (Dorléac)

Kevin Spacey (Fowler)

Beck Hansen (Campbell)

Elvis Costello (MacManus)

Ian Holm (Cuthbert)

Klaus Maria Brandauer (Steng)

Men Who Can Use the Roman Numeral III After Their Name

Ted Turner, Davis Love, Ted Danson, Alec Baldwin, Cliff Robertson, Luke Perry, Bill Gates, Eminem (Marshall Mathers III), Sam Shepard (born Samuel Shepard Rogers III), London Wainwright (he does use it)

People Who Adopted Children

Ellen Burstyn, Tom Hanks, Angelina Jolie, Ilie Nastase, Ronald Reagan, Lionel Richie, Marlon Brando, Burt Reynolds and Loni Anderson, Linda Ronstadt, Sheena Easton, Steven Spielberg and Kate Capshaw, Burt Bacharach and Carole Bayer Sager, Jill Ireland and Charles

Bronson, Ted Danson, Graham Chapman, Magic Johnson, Muhammad Ali, David Niven, Henry Fonda, Rosie O'Donnell, Isabella Rossellini, Robin Givens, Ella Fitzgerald, Kate Jackson, John Denver, Joan Crawford, George Burns, Patti LaBelle, Walt Disney, James Cagney, Bob Hope, Jerry Lewis, Paul Newman and Joanne Woodward, Bette Davis, Josephine Baker, Imelda Marcos, Harpo Marx, Hugh Jackman, Brian Dennehy, Sharon Stone

People with Famous Stepparents

Sally Field—Jock Mahoney

David Cassidy—Shirley Jones

Paloma Picasso—Jonas Salk

Nicolette Sheridan—Telly Savalas

Christian Bale—Gloria Steinem

Carlene Carter—Johnny Cash

Liv Tyler—Todd Rundgren

Bijou Phillips—Michelle Phillips

N.B.: Gore Vidal shared a stepfather with Jacqueline Kennedy (his mother, Nina, married Jackie's stepfather, Hugh Auchincloss)

Baby-Sitters

Little Eva baby-sat for Carole King's children—which is how she came to sing Carole King's hit "The Locomotion."

Lindsay Wagner baby-sat for Glen Campbell's children.

Billy Crystal had Billie Holiday as a baby-sitter.

Edward Norton had Betsy True as a baby-sitter.

Car Acronyms

AUDI
Accelerates Under Demonic Influence
Always Unsafe Designs Implemented

BMW
Born Moderately Wealthy
Break My Windows
Bought My Wife

BUICK
Big, Ugly, Indestructible Car Killer

CHEVROLET
Car Has Extensive Valve Rattle On Long, Extended Trips
Cheap, Hardly Efficient, Virtually Runs On Luck Every
Time

CHEVY
Cheapest Heap Ever Visioned Yet

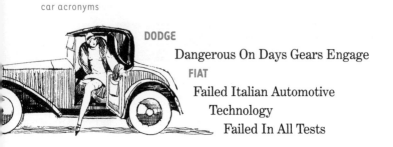

DODGE

Dangerous On Days Gears Engage

FIAT

Failed Italian Automotive
Technology
Failed In All Tests

FORD

Fix Or Repair Daily

Fails On Rainy Days

Fast Only Rolling Downhill

HONDA

Had One—Never Did Again

HYUNDAI

Hope You Understand Nothing's Drivable And
Inexpensive

MAZDA

Most Always Zipping Dangerously Along

MERCEDES

Many Expensive Repairs Can Eventually Discourage
Extra Sales

NISSAN

Needs Immediate Salvage So Abandon Now

OLDSMOBILE

Overpriced, Leisurely Driven Sedan Made Of Buick's
Irregular Leftover Equipment

PONTIAC

Poor Old Nut Thinks It's A Cadillac

PORSCHE

Proof Only Rich Suckers Can Have Everything

ROLLS-ROYCE
Regarded Only as Luxury Life Style—
Runs Over Your Current Expenses

SAAB
Sad Attempt At Beauty
Send Another Automobile Back

SUBARU
Screwed Up Beyond All Repair Usually

TOYOTA
Too Often Yanks Overprice This Auto

VOLVO
Very Odd-Looking Vehicular Object

Harley-Davidson Owners

Arnold Schwarzenegger, Whitney Houston, Burt Reynolds, Eric Clapton, Sylvester Stallone, Billy Idol, Jon Bon Jovi, Wynonna, Liam Neeson, George Clooney, Bruce Willis, Damon Hill, David Copperfield, Ronan Keating, Kurt Russell, Colin Farrell, Steve McQueen, Jim Bowen, Errol Flynn, Elvis Presley, T. E. Lawrence, Bill Haley, George Sanders, Clark Gable, Howard Hughes

Survived a Helicopter Crash

Christie Brinkley, Kirk Douglas, Leni Riefenstahl (at the age of ninety-seven)

Astronomy

Buzz Aldrin's mother's maiden name was Moon.

The Sun is 93 million miles from Earth, which is 270 times closer than the next-nearest star.

A car traveling at 100 miles per hour would take more than 29 million years to reach the next-nearest star—but you could reach the Sun by car in a little over 106 years.

It would take about 2,000 years to walk to the Sun.

Since the Moon has no atmosphere, footprints left there by astronauts will remain visible for at least 10 million years.

All the planets in our solar system could be placed inside the planet Jupiter.

All the moons of the solar system are named after Greek and Roman mythology, except the moons of Uranus, which are named after Shakespearean characters.

If you take a pound of cobwebs and spread them out in a straight line, it will go twice around the Earth.

Neutron stars are so condensed that a fragment the size of a sugar cube would weigh as much as all the people on Earth put together.

A lightning bolt generates temperatures 5 times hotter than those found at the Sun's surface.

Over a thousand planets the size of the Earth could fit inside the Sun.

If you were standing on Mercury, the Sun would appear 2.5 times larger than it appears on Earth.

Uranus is visible to the naked eye.

It takes 8.5 minutes for light to get from the Sun to the Earth.

The Milky Way galaxy contains 5 billion stars larger than our Sun.

The Earth weighs approximately 6,588,000,000,000,000,000 tons.

Ten tons of space dust fall on the Earth every day.

Every year the Sun loses 360 million tons.

The pressure at the Earth's inner core is 3 million times the Earth's atmospheric pressure.

When the Americans sent a man into space, they spent a million dollars developing a pen that could write upside down in conditions of zero gravity. The Russians used a pencil.

The average modern home computer is more powerful than all of NASA's computers at the time of the Apollo moon landings put together.

In 1963, baseball pitcher **Gaylord Perry** remarked, "They'll put a man on the moon before I hit a home run." On July 20, 1969, a few hours after Neil Armstrong set foot on the moon, Gaylord Perry hit his first—and only—home run.

N.B.: The Mount of Jupiter and the Girdle of Venus are found on the palm of your hand.

Number 142,857

142,857 is a cyclic number: when multiplied by any other number, it will produce a number containing the same digits *in the same order*—albeit starting in a different place.

1 x 142,857 = 142,857
2 x 142,857 = 285,714
3 x 142,857 = 428,571
4 x 142,857 = 571,428
5 x 142,857 = 714,285
6 x 142,857 = 857,142

Look what happens when you multiply 142,857 by 7: it equals 999,999.

When 1 is divided by 7, it comes to 0.142857,142857,142857.

If you multiply 142,857 by 8, you get 1,142,856. If you take off the first digit (1) and add it to the last six digits, see what happens: 1 + 142,856 = 142,857.

Similarly, if you multiply 142,857 by, say, 17, you get 2,428,569. Now take off the first digit (2) and add it to the last six digits and see what happens: 2 + 428,569 = 428,571—which is, of course, the original number in stage three of its cycle.

You can do this with every number except multiples of 7 (although these also produce interesting results).

If you take the number 142,857 and split it into two—142 and 857—and then add those two numbers, you get 999.

More Numbers

Japanese researchers have calculated pi to 1.2411 trillion places. If you need to remember pi, just count the letters in each word of the sentence "May I have a large container of coffee?" If you get the coffee and are polite, say, "Thank you," get two more decimal places: 3.141592653 . . .

The 772nd to 777th digits of pi are 999999.

For the ancient Greeks, any number more than 10,000 was a "myriad."

When 21,978 is multiplied by 4, the result is 87,912—which is 21,978 reversed.

171

Any number, squared, is equal to one more than the numbers on either side of it multiplied together: $5 \times 5 = 25$ and $4 \times 6 = 24$; $6 \times 6 = 36$ and $5 \times 7 = 35$, et cetera.

The Roman numerals for 1,666 are MDCLXVI (1,000+500+100+50+10+5+1)—the only year featuring all the Roman numerals from the highest to the lowest.

One penny doubled every day becomes over £5 million in just 30 days.

$37 \times 3 = 111$
$37 \times 6 = 222$
$37 \times 9 = 333$
$37 \times 12 = 444$
$37 \times 15 = 555$
$37 \times 18 = 666$
$37 \times 21 = 777$

If you add up the numbers 1 to 100 consecutively $(1 + 2 + 3 + 4 + 5$, etc.) the total is 5,050.

The most recent year that could be written both upside down and right side up and appear the same was 1961. The next year this will be possible will be 6009.

The smallest number with three letters is 1

... with four letters is 4
... with five letters is 3
... with six letters is 11
... with seven letters is 15
... with eight letters is 13

. . . with nine letters is 17

. . . with 10 letters is 24

The word **INTERCHANGEABILITY** contains the numbers THREE, EIGHT, NINE, TEN, THIRTEEN, THIRTY, THIRTY-NINE, EIGHTY, EIGHTY-NINE, NINETY and NINETY-EIGHT

In English, the only number that has the same number of letters as its name is FOUR. Here are some other languages and the only numbers that contain precisely the same number of letters:

Basque BEDERATZI (9)

Catalan U (1)

Czech TRI (3)

Danish and Norwegian TO (2), TRE (3), FIRE (4)

Dutch VIER (4)

Esperanto DU (2), TRI (3), KVAR (4)

Finnish VIISI (5)

German VIER (4)

Italian TRE (3)

Pilipino APAT (4)

Polish PIATY (5)

Portuguese and Spanish CINCO (5)

Romanian CINCI (5)

Serbo-Croatian TRI (3)

Swedish TRE (3), FYRA (4)

Turkish DÖRT (4)

The word **THOUSAND** contains the letter A, but none of the words for numbers from 1 to 999 has an A.

Two of a Kind

DIED IN AN APARTMENT OWNED BY HARRY NILSSON
Mama Cass Elliot
Keith Moon

OWNS A STUD FARM
Charlie Watts
Susan George

HAS EYES OF DIFFERENT COLORS
Jane Seymour (one green and one brown)
David Bowie (one green and one blue)

MARRIED A WOMAN NAMED KELLY PRESTON (NOT THE SAME WOMAN)
Lou Diamond Phillips
John Travolta

MODELED FOR TEEN PHOTO-ROMANCE STORIES
Hugh Grant
George Michael

Queen Elizabeth II

The Queen was the first future monarch to be born in a private house—17 Bruton Street, London W1—which is now the site of a bank. She was delivered by caesarean section on a Wednesday.

When she was born, she was third in line to the throne (her father and her uncle David, later King Edward VIII, were ahead of her).

She learned to curtsy perfectly before the age of two and made her last curtsy in 1952, to her father's body in St. George's Chapel, Windsor.

She's five feet four inches and weighs about 112 pounds.

She and Prince Philip were related before they married. They're third cousins (through their descent from Queen Victoria) and second cousins once removed (through King Christian IX of Denmark).

The Queen has only once signed an autograph for a member of the public. In 1945, Sergeant Pat Hayes asked for her autograph and was given it.

Her childhood nickname was "Lilibet," which was the way she mispronounced her own name and is now the name by which her closest relatives know her; her grandmother, Queen Mary, called her "the bambino."

At the precise moment in 1952 when she acceded to the throne, she was wearing a shirt, a cardigan and a pair of slacks.

She's superstitious: she throws salt over her left shoulder if she accidentally spills any, she won't have thirteen people at the dinner table, and she's been known to touch wood before her horses run.

Whenever she travels abroad, she always takes with her barley water, a specially formulated egg-and-lemon shampoo and her feather pillow.

As Queen, she can or could: drive without taking a driving test; disobey the laws of the land, because they are, of course, *her* laws; refuse to give evidence in court, as the courts are *her* courts (she also can't be sued); declare war on another country (the armed forces are under her command); disband the army and sell all the navy's ships; send letters without putting stamps on (her letters carry the royal cipher); give as many honors—including peerages and knighthoods—as she likes; declare a state of emergency (which she once did—on May 31, 1955, because of the railway strike); turn any parish in the country into a university; pardon any (or all) of the prisoners in *her* jails; dismiss the government, and get rid of the civil service.

The Queen's retinue includes the Keeper of the Queen's Swans, the Mistress of the Robes, the Queen's Raven Master, the Clerk of the Closet, the Lady of the Bedchamber, the Woman of the Bedchamber, the Hereditary Grand Falconer, the Royal Bargemaster, the Queen's Racing Pigeon Manager and the Grand Almoner.

The Queen loves military march music, popular classical works and musicals, champagne, corgis, watching TV, horse racing, crossword puzzles, impersonations (she's also a gifted impressionist herself) and charades.

The Queen hates dictating letters, garlic, cats, tennis, pomposity, the cold, smoking and any mention of

King Edward VIII, whose abdication pushed her father onto the throne, the stress of which (or so her mother always believed) caused his early death.

Titles Held by Prince Philip

Privy Councillor, Knight of the Thistle, Admiral of the Royal Yacht Squadron, Grand Master of the Guild of Air Pilots and Air Navigators, Field-Marshal, Marshal of the RAF, Admiral of the Fleet, Knight of the Garter, Chancellor of the University of Cambridge

The Way We Live

Ninety percent of women who walk into a department store immediately turn to the right. No one knows why.

Tuesday is the most productive day of the workweek.

A total of 908,000 U.S. dollar bills weigh exactly a ton.

The average woman uses about 6 pounds of lipstick during her lifetime.

It is estimated that at any one time, 0.7 percent of the world's population is intoxicated.

There has never been a sex-change operation performed in Ireland.

Ninety percent of movies released in the United States are porn films.

Couples who marry in January, February or March have the highest divorce rate.

Seventy-five percent of Japanese women own vibrators. The global average is 47 percent.

The Christmas holidays are the busiest time in plastic surgeons' offices.

Eighty percent of women wash their hands after leaving a public toilet; only 55 percent of men do.

In Turkey, the color of mourning is violet. In most Muslim countries and in China, it is white.

In China, the bride wears red.

Forty percent of people who come to a party in your home take a peek in your medicine cabinet.

One in every 8 boss-secretary romances ends in marriage.

Twenty-five percent of all businesses in the United States are franchises.

People who work at night tend to weigh more than people who work during the day.

On an average workday, a typist's fingers travel 12.6 miles.

On average, Americans stand 14 inches apart when they converse.

One out of 5 pieces of the world's garbage is generated in the United States.

Six percent of American men propose marriage by phone.

There's an average of 178 sesame seeds on a Big Mac bun.

About 75 percent of the people in the United States live on 2 percent of the land.

In the vast majority of the world's languages, the word for "mother" begins with the letter m.

Mexico City has more taxis than any other city in the world.

Eighty-five percent of international phone calls are conducted in English.

The largest toy distributor in the world is McDonald's.

The average person drinks 70,000 cups of coffee in a lifetime.

After a 3-week vacation, your IQ can drop by as much as 20 percent.

In the course of a lifetime, the average person spends about 2 years on the phone.

The typical driver will honk a car horn 15,250 times during his or her lifetime.

The average British adult will eat 35,000 biscuits in a lifetime.

In the United States, 9 milligrams of rat droppings are allowed in a kilogram of wheat.

Every year, the average person eats 428 bugs by mistake.

One in every 4 Americans has appeared on television.

Every year, 8,000 people injure themselves while using a toothpick.

On average, when asked for a color, 3 out of 5 people will say red.

Peanuts are one of the ingredients of dynamite.

Thirty percent of all the nonbiodegradable trash buried in American landfills is disposable diapers.

The stall closest to the door in a public toilet is the cleanest, because it is the least used.

People spend 2 weeks of their lives kissing.

People spend more than 5 years of their lives dreaming.

A typist's left hand does 56 percent of the work.

The average driver will be locked out of his or her car nine times during the course of a lifetime.

Yoga Practitioners

Geri Halliwell, Ali MacGraw, Gillian Anderson, Jerry Hall, Sting, Trudie Styler, Woody Harrelson, Goldie Hawn, Madonna, Gwyneth Paltrow, Raquel Welch, Brooke Shields, Michael Jackson, Patricia Arquette, Al Pacino, Flea, Courtney Love, Jodie Foster, Cindy Crawford, Ricky Martin, Helen Hunt, Jerry Seinfeld, Mel C, Kristin Davis, Tobey Maguire, Justin Timberlake, Reese Witherspoon, Rachel Weisz, Heather Graham, Demi Moore, James Spader

Eyes Corrected by Laser Surgery

Richard Branson, Courteney Cox, Tiger Woods, Brad Pitt, Julianne Moore, Nicole Kidman, Adam Sandler, Sally Jessy Raphael, Ewan McGregor, Elton John

Used HRT (Hormone Replacement Therapy)

Joan Collins, Germaine Greer, Stephanie Beacham, Anne Robinson

Had a Vasectomy

Dean Martin, Faron Young, Billy Eckstine, Abbie Hoffman, Howard Hughes

Had a Liver Transplant

George Best, Larry Hagman, Jack Bruce, David Crosby, Rory Gallagher

Flat Feet

Newt Gingrich, Prince Charles, Cyndi Lauper, Stephen King, Terence Stamp

Hard of Hearing

David Hockney, Lester Piggott, Bill Clinton, Norman Mailer, King Juan Carlos, Rob Lowe (deaf in his right ear), Luciano Pavarotti, Stephanie Beacham, George Martin, Brian Wilson (deaf in one ear and so has never heard his songs in stereo), Halle Berry (lost 80 percent hearing in her left ear after ex-lover beat her), Richard Thomas

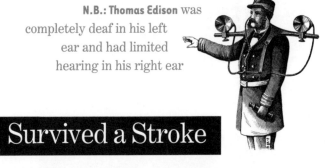

N.B.: Thomas Edison was completely deaf in his left ear and had limited hearing in his right ear

Survived a Stroke

Kirk Douglas, Boris Yeltsin, Sharon Stone

Had Kidney Stones

Bob Dole, Montserrat Caballé, Michael Crawford, Richard Attenborough, Steve Cram

Had Appendix Removed

Dave Stewart (unnecessarily so—it was just gas), Dian Fossey (as a precaution before going into the jungle), Mel Gibson, Pope John Paul II, Fidel Castro, Jenna Bush, Minnie Driver, Kelsey Grammer, Tim Allen, Glenda Jackson, Prince Charles, Kevin Costner, Julia Volkova (of Tatu), Kate Beckinsale

Had Tonsils Removed as an Adult

Ringo Starr, Bryan Ferry, Drew Barrymore, Rudolf Nureyev

Heart Murmur

Arnold Schwarzenegger, Bridget Fonda, Retief Goosen, Rachel Hunter, Evander Holyfield, Elizabeth Taylor

Has a Heart Pacemaker

Elton John, Dick Cheney, Roger Moore

Had Epilepsy

Julius Caesar, Alexander the Great, Vincent van Gogh, Peter the Great, Billy Idol, Neil Young, Ward Bond, Margaux Hemingway, Florence Griffith Joyner, Elton John, Bud Abbott, Napoleon, Richard Burton, Leonardo da Vinci, Charles Dickens, Hugo Weaving

Survived Meningitis

Victoria Beckham, Jerry Lewis, Queen Beatrix of the Netherlands, Steve Elkington, Maria Shriver, Johnny Rotten (Lydon)

Tinnitus Sufferers

Pete Townshend, Barbra Streisand, Jack Straw

Suffered from Asthma

Steven Seagal, Wynonna, Stephen Fry, Joe Jackson (used to be put into oxygen tents in hospital), Kathleen Quinlan

Suffered from Anorexia

Karen Carpenter, Kate Beckinsale, Sandra Dee

Suffered from Bulimia

Princess Diana, Zina Garrison, Uri Geller, Jane Fonda, Emma Thompson, Elton John, Geri Halliwell, Carré Otis

Suffer from Parkinson's Disease

Michael J. Fox, Muhammad Ali, Janet Reno, Deborah Kerr, Billy Graham

Suffered from Manic Depression

Axl Rose, Vincent van Gogh, Ted Turner, Vivien Leigh, Robert Schumann, Abbie Hoffman, Margot Kidder, Mario Lanza, Capucine, Dorothy Dandridge, Patty Duke

Suffered from Childhood Polio

Alan Alda, Joni Mitchell, Neil Young, Itzhak Perlman, Wilma Rudolph, Dinah Shore, Francis Ford Coppola

Diabetics

Luther Vandross, Mary Tyler Moore, Halle Berry, Steven Redgrave, Mick Fleetwood, Sharon Stone, B. B. King, George Lucas, Meat Loaf, Brian Cox

Survived a Heart Attack

Edward Woodward, Martin Sheen, Kerry Packer, Omar Sharif, Eddy Grant, Jerry Lee Lewis

Suffer from Arthritis

John Cleese, Queen Elizabeth II, José Maria Olazabal, Elizabeth Taylor, Prince Philip, Jack Nicklaus, Barry Gibb

Survived a Nervous Breakdown

Emily Lloyd, David Helfgott, Bob Hoskins, Yitzhak Rabin, Leslie Caron, Brian Wilson, Daniel Day-Lewis, Yves Saint Laurent, Kylie Minogue, Lee Evans, Roseanne, Tuesday Weld, Mariah Carey, Beyoncé Knowles, Kate Beckinsale

187

Lost a Finger

Jerry Garcia, Boris Yeltsin, James Doohan, Dr. Alex Comfort, Telly Savalas, Daryl Hannah (wears a prosthetic fingertip), Isoroku Yamamoto (the admiral who planned the attack on Pearl Harbor), Matt Perry (lost middle finger in kindergarten accident), Gary Burghoff (Radar from *M*A*S*H*—left hand always hidden on camera), Dustin Hoffman (lost the tip of his finger when a seat collapsed while filming *Finding Neverland* in 2003)

Blind

Stevie Wonder, Ray Charles, Louis Braille, Claude Monet, Helen Keller, Jose Feliciano, James Thurber, Joseph Pulitzer, George Shearing

Lost an Eye

Gordon Banks, Rex Harrison, John Ford, Moshe Dayan, Peter Falk, Sammy Davis Jr., Sandy Duncan, Alan Jay Lerner, Raoul Walsh, Ry Cooder

Have Used Viagra

Jim Carrey, Jerry Springer, Bob Dole, Hugh Hefner, Julio Iglesias, Ryan O'Neal, Vidal Sassoon, Ben Affleck (once—"All it did was make me sweat and feel dizzy. I felt no sexual effects whatsoever"), Kim Cattrall, Jack Nicholson, Ozzy Osbourne

Pregnancy Cravings

Catherine Zeta-Jones—beetroot (first child), Branston pickle and curry (second child)

Mel B—peanut butter, cheesecake, ice cream and french fries

Gloria Estefan—sweetened condensed milk

Victoria Beckham—gherkins

Kate Winslet—fizzy cola candies, blackcurrant juice and tomatoes

Madonna—butternut squash

Marie Osmond—grapefruit sorbet topped with sardines

Cate Blanchett—sardines

Brooke Shields—extremely strong coffee and nutmeg

Ms. Dynamite—strawberry-flavor Ben & Jerry's ice cream

Nature

Millions of trees are accidentally planted by squirrels that bury nuts and then forget where they left them.

The smallest trees in the world are Greenland dwarf willows.

It snowed in the Sahara Desert on February 18, 1979.

The canopy of a rain forest is so thick that only 1 percent of sunlight reaches the ground.

An ordinary raindrop falls at about 7 miles per hour.

Heavy rain pours down at the rate of about 20 miles per hour.

Lightning strikes the Earth about 200 times a second.

The Siberian larch accounts for more than 20 percent of the world's trees.

The giant water lily grows almost a foot a day.

Some bamboo plants grow 3 feet a day.

Oak trees do not produce acorns until they are at least 50 years old.

A cucumber is 96 percent water.

There is cyanide in apple seeds.

A notch in a tree will remain the same distance from the ground as the tree grows.

If you put a raisin in a glass of champagne, it will keep floating to the top and sinking to the bottom.

Almonds are part of the peach family.

There are more stars in the universe than grains of sand on all the beaches in the world.

There are 10 million bacteria in a liter of milk; that's equivalent to the population of Greece.

Cranberries are one of just 3 major fruits native to North America. Blueberries and Concord grapes are the others.

A ripe cranberry will bounce.

Wheat is the world's most widely cultivated plant, grown on every continent except Antarctica.

All snow crystals are hexagonal.

The water we drink is 3 billion years old.

The average iceberg weighs 20 million tons.

You can figure out which way is south if you are near a tree stump. The growth rings are wider on the south side.

It is estimated that a plastic container can resist decomposition for as long as 50,000 years.

The most abundant metal in the Earth's crust is aluminum. The Chinese were using aluminum to make things as early as A.D. 300. Western civilization didn't rediscover it until 1827.

The angle of the branches from the trunk of a tree is constant from one member to another of the same species.

The cashew is a member of the poison ivy family.

Strawberries are a member of the rose family.

Most orchids are bisexual.

Science

If you slowly pour a handful of salt into a totally full glass of water, it will not overflow. In fact, the water level will go down.

Hot water freezes more quickly than cold water.

Magnesium was used in early flash photography because it burns with a brilliant light.

A scientific satellite needs only 250 watts of power to operate.

Minus 40 degrees Celsius is exactly the same temperature as minus 40 degrees Fahrenheit.

Radio waves travel so much faster than sound waves that a broadcast voice can be heard sooner 18,000 kilometers away than in the back of the room in which it originated.

Waves break when their height reaches more than seven-tenths of the depth of the water.

X-ray technology has shown that there are 3 different versions of *The Mona Lisa* under the one that's visible.

In an atom, the weight of an electron is 1/1850 of a proton.

At the deepest point of the ocean (11.034 kilometers), an iron ball would take more than an hour to sink to the ocean floor.

When scientists at Australia's Parkes Observatory began picking up radio waves, they thought they had proof of alien life. However, it transpired that the emissions came from a microwave oven in the building.

Only 13.5 percent of scientists are women.

Sterling silver contains 7.5 percent copper.

Hydrogen gas is the least dense substance.

Ocean waves can travel as fast as a jet plane.

Aspirin was the first drug offered as a water-soluble tablet, in 1900.

Mercury is the only metal that is liquid at room temperature.

In a scientific study, children were told to imagine that they were wearing heavy mittens. The temperature of their fingertips went up.

One twenty-fifth of the energy put out by a lightbulb is light. The rest is heat.

No matter how high or low it flies, an airplane's shadow is always the same size.

Because of the rotation of the Earth, an object can be thrown farther if it is thrown west.

Guest Appearances on TV Programs

ABSOLUTELY FABULOUS

Germaine Greer, Richard E. Grant, Marianne Faithfull, Zandra Rhodes, Britt Ekland, Christian Lacroix, Whoopi Goldberg, Debbie Harry, Kristin Scott, Lulu Thomas, Minnie Driver, Emma Bunton, Elton John

CHEERS

Glynis Johns, Dick Cavett, Sherilyn Fenn, Gary Hart, Lisa Kudrow, Arsenio Hall, Bobby Hatfield, Michael Dukakis, Celeste Holm, Harry Connick Jr., Harvey Fierstein, John Kerry, Johnny Carson

M*A*S*H

Leslie Nielsen, Ron Howard, Loudon Wainwright III, Brian Dennehy

"PHONED UP" FRASIER

Mel Brooks, Rosemary Clooney, Jeff Daniels, Patty Hearst, Piper Laurie, Timothy Leary, John Malkovich, Henry Mancini, Joe Mantegna, Reba McEntire, Mary Tyler Moore, Christopher Reeve, Carl

Reiner, Eric Stoltz, Garry Trudeau, Eddie Van Halen, Elijah Wood, Amy Madigan, Art Garfunkel, Ben Stiller, Beverly D'Angelo, Billy Crystal, Carrie Fisher, Cindy Crawford, Cyd Charisse, David Duchovny, Ed Harris, Eric Idle, Gillian Anderson, Gloria Estefan, Halle Berry, Jay Leno, Jill Clayburgh, Joan Allen, JoBeth Williams, Jodie Foster, John Cusack, John Lithgow, John McEnroe, Kevin Bacon, Laura Dern, Lily Tomlin, Macaulay Culkin, Mary Elizabeth Mastrantonio, Matthew Broderick, Pia Zadora, Ron Howard, Sandra Dee, Shelley Duvall, Tom Hulce, Tommy Hilfiger, William H. Macy, Yo-Yo Ma

GUESTED ON *FRIENDS*

George Clooney (Dr. Mitchell)

Julia Roberts (Susie Moss)

Elliott Gould (Jack Geller—Monica and Ross's father)

Noah Wyle (Dr. Rosen)

Chris Isaak (Rob Donnen—children's library organizer)

Tom Selleck (Dr. Richard Burke—Monica's boyfriend)

Morgan Fairchild (Nora Bing—Chandler's mother)

Brooke Shields (Erika Ford—Joey's stalker)

Jean-Claude Van Damme (as himself)

Charlie Sheen (Ryan—Phoebe's sailor)

Charlton Heston (as himself)

The Duchess of York (as herself)

Jennifer Saunders (Mrs. Waltham—Emily's stepmother)

Tom Conti (Dr. Waltham—Emily's father)

Richard Branson (as himself)

Robin Williams (Thomas)

Billy Crystal (Tim)

David Arquette (Malcolm—Ursula's stalker)

Hank Azaria (David—Phoebe's scientist boyfriend)

Elle Macpherson (Janine Lacroix—Joey's roommate)

Sherilyn Fenn (Ginger—the girl with the wooden leg)

Helen Hunt (Jamie Buchanan)

Chrissie Hynde (Stephanie—a professional guitarist)

Ralph Lauren (as himself)

Jay Leno (as himself)

Rebecca Romijn-Stamos (Cheryl—Ross's girlfriend)

Isabella Rossellini (as herself)

Ben Stiller (Tommy—Rachel's boyfriend)

Bruce Willis (Paul Stevens—Elizabeth's father and Rachel's boyfriend)

Reese Witherspoon (Jill Greene—Rachel's sister)

GUESTED ON *STAR TREK*

Joan Collins, Stephanie Beacham, Whoopi Goldberg, Teri Garr, Linda Thorson, Kelsey Grammer, Stephen Hawking, Steven Berkoff, Mick Fleetwood, David Soul, Iggy Pop, King Abdullah of Jordan (had a cameo, nonspeaking role)

Great Misquotations

"I never said I want to be alone, I only said I want to be *left* alone." (Greta Garbo)

(Wrong quotation followed by correct one)

"Alas, poor Yorick, I knew him well."

"Alas poor Yorick! I knew him, Horatio." (Hamlet in *Hamlet* by William Shakespeare)

"A little knowledge is a dangerous thing."

"A little learning is a dangerous thing." (Alexander Pope)

"Spare the rod, spoil the child."

"He who spares the rod hates his son, but he who loves him is careful to discipline him." (The Bible)

"Money is the root of all evil."

"For the love of money is the root of all evil." (The Bible)

"Abandon hope, all ye who enter here."

"Abandon all hope, you who enter." (*The Divine Comedy* by Dante)

"Water, water everywhere, and not a drop to drink."

"Water, water everywhere, nor any drop to drink." (The *Rime of the Ancient Mariner* by Samuel T. Coleridge)

"Hell hath no fury like a woman scorned."

"Heaven has no rage like love to hatred turned, / Nor hell a fury like a woman scorned." (*The Mourning Bride* by William Congreve)

"Music has charms to soothe a savage beast."

"Music has charms to soothe a savage breast." (*The Mourning Bride* by William Congreve)

"Come up and see me sometime."

"Why don't you come up sometime, and see me?" (Mae West to Cary Grant in *She Done Him Wrong*)

"Pride goes before a fall."

"Pride goeth before destruction and an haughty spirit before a fall." (The Bible)

"My lips are sealed."

"My lips are not yet unsealed." (Stanley Baldwin)

"Nice guys finish last."

"Nice guys finish seventh." (Brooklyn Dodgers manager Leo Durocher, speaking in the days when the National League had seven teams, so seventh was, in fact, last)

"Elementary, my dear Watson."

"Elementary." (Sherlock Holmes to Dr. Watson in Sir Arthur Conan Doyle's stories)

"Hubble bubble, toil and trouble."

"Double double, toil and trouble." (The witches in *Macbeth* by William Shakespeare)

"Methinks the lady doth protest too much."

"The lady does protest too much, methinks." (Gertrude in *Hamlet* by William Shakespeare)

"To gild the lily."

"To gild refined gold, to paint the lily." (The Earl of Salisbury in *King John* by William Shakespeare)

"Me Tarzan, you Jane."

Tarzan and Jane pointed at themselves, and they each said their own name in *Tarzan the Ape Man*

"He who hesitates is lost."

"The woman that deliberates is lost." (*Cato* by Joseph Addison)

"Et tu, Brutus?"

"Et tu, Brute?" (Julius Caesar. In the unlikely event that he said those words, Brutus would have taken the vocative.)

"When in Rome, do as the Romans do."

"If you are at Rome, live after the Roman fashion; if you are elsewhere, live as they do there." (St. Ambrose)

"I disapprove of what you say, but I will defend to the death your right to say it."

"Think for yourselves, and let others enjoy the privilege to do so, too." (Voltaire)

"Don't look a gift horse the mouth."

"Never inspect the teeth of a gift horse." (Original proverb)

"Discretion is the better part of valor."

"The better part of valor is discretion." (Falstaff in *King Henry IV, Part I* by William Shakespeare)

"There's method in his madness."

"Though this be madness, yet there is method in't." (Polonius in *Hamlet* by William Shakespeare)

"In the future, everybody will be famous for fifteen minutes."

"In the future, there won't be any more stars. TV will be so accessible that everybody will be a star for fifteen minutes." (Andy Warhol)

People and the Films They Directed

Norman Mailer—*Tough Guys Don't Dance* (1987)

Frank Sinatra—*None But the Brave* (1965)

Joan Rivers—*Rabbit Test* (1978)

Anthony Quinn—*The Buccaneer* (1958)

Rossano Brazzi—*The Christmas That Almost Wasn't* (1966)

James Clavell—*To Sir, with Love* (1967)

Arnold Schwarzenegger—*Christmas in Connecticut* (1992)

Michael Crichton—*Westworld* (1973)

Albert Finney—*Charlie Bubbles* (1968)

Patrick McGoohan—*Catch My Soul* (1973)

Timothy Leary—*Cheech and Chong's Nice Dream* (1981)

Tom Stoppard—*Rosencrantz & Guildenstern Are Dead* (1990)

Michael Nesmith—*Doctor Duck's Super Secret All-Purpose Sauce* (1985)

Ringo Starr—*Born to Boogie* (1972)

201

Howard Hughes—*Hell's Angels* (1930)

Larry Hagman—*Son of Blob* (1972)

Richard Burton—*Dr. Faustus* (1967)

Songs That Inspired Films

"Coward of the County": Kenny Rogers's 1980 hit about a supposed coward who eventually learns to fight became a 1981 film starring Mr. Rogers himself as a preacher whose nephew is the "coward."

"Convoy": Back in 1976, at the height of the CB-radio craze, C. W. McCall released "Convoy," about a trucker trying to run a police blockade. Two years later, Sam Peckinpah directed a film based on the song, starring Kris Kristofferson and Ali MacGraw.

"Torn Between Two Lovers": In 1977, Mary MacGregor had a Top 5 hit with this ballad. In a 1979 film of the same name, Lee Remick is similarly torn between George Peppard and Joseph Bologna.

"Rock Around the Clock": Bill Haley and his Comets' hit record caused teenagers to rip up theater seats when it was featured in the credits of the 1955 film *The Blackboard Jungle.* The following year, Bill and the boys starred in a cheap film named after their classic song.

"Mrs. Brown, You've Got a Lovely Daughter": In 1965, Herman's Hermits had a U.S. #1 with this song. Three years later, the lads were cast in a film of the same name, which attempted to cash in on the Swinging London phenomenon.

"Harper Valley PTA": In 1968, Jeannie C. Riley had a hit with this song about a woman who is ruled to be an unfit mother by her local PTA. The 1978 film of the same name—starring Barbara Eden—took this story and showed the heroine getting even by exposing the members of the PTA as hypocrites.

"Yellow Submarine": The 1966 Beatles song—the only single to feature Ringo on lead vocals—was the inspiration for the 1968 animated film (cowritten by *Love Story* author Erich Segal), which has become a cult classic.

"Ode to Billy Joe": In 1967, Bobbie Gentry released this song about a love affair that ends in suicide. In 1976, a film of the same title opened up the story of Billy Joe and his jump off the Tallahatchee Bridge.

"Lili Marlene": This extraordinary song's place in musical history was assured when it became the only song in World War II to be adopted by both the Germans and the British. The song subsequently inspired a 1980 film of the same name, starring Hanna Schygulla.

"White Christmas": The song "White Christmas"—
written by Irving Berlin—was so popular when Bing
Crosby sang it in the 1942 film *Holiday Inn* that it
was used as the title of a 1954 film—also starring
Bing Crosby.

People and the Films They Appeared In

Martin Amis—*A High Wind in Jamaica*

Björk—*Dancer in the Dark*

Anna Kournikova—*Me, Myself and Irene*

Naomi Campbell—*Girl 6*

Sergio Garcia—*Stuck on You*

Bruce Springsteen—*High Fidelity*

Jackie Collins—*All at Sea*

Craig Stadler—*Tin Cup*

Herb Alpert—*The Ten Commandments*

Magic Johnson—*Grand Canyon*

Ernest Hemingway—*The Old Man and the Sea*

Justin Timberlake—*Model Behavior*

Germaine Greer—*Universal Soldier*

John McEnroe—*Anger Management*

Pablo Picasso—*Life Begins Tomorrow*

Leon Trotsky—*My Official Wife*

Saul Bellow—*Zelig*

Mark Twain—*A Curious Dream*

Graham Greene—*Day for Night*

Elle Macpherson—*Sirens*

Yoko Ono—*Satan's Bed*

Walt Disney

Born on December 5, 1901, Walt(er) Elias Disney first started drawing cartoons professionally in exchange for free haircuts.

When he was sixteen, Disney tried to enlist in the U.S. Army but was refused admission because of his age. So he tried the Canadian army—with the same result. Eventually he went to France as a Red Cross ambulance driver.

While waiting to become an ambulance driver, he worked as a postal clerk in Chicago. When he returned from France, he worked as a postal clerk in Kansas City.

Disney started the Laugh-O-Gram Corporation, a vehicle for his animated fairy tales, in Kansas City in 1921 with $15,000 from investors. He went bankrupt two years later, when his backers pulled out as a result of problems with New York distributors.

In 1923, he went to Hollywood to go into partnership with his brother Roy, taking all his worldly possessions: one jacket, one pair of trousers, one shirt, two sets of underwear and a few drawing materials.

For four years, Disney and his wife, the actress Lillian Bounds, lived in poverty, until he had a (relative) success with *Oswald the Lucky Rabbit.*

The same year, Disney took inspiration from the mice that used to play in his studio and created Mickey Mouse. He originally called him "Mortimer," but his wife thought "Mickey" sounded better. Disney himself supplied the voice for Mickey in the 1928 hit talkie *Steamboat Willie.* Disney once said of his creation, "I love Mickey more than any woman I've ever known."

Disney's 1940 film *Pinocchio* is regarded as a classic, but Paulo Lorenzini, the nephew of the original author of *Pinocchio,* Carlo Lorenzini, wanted the Italian government to sue Disney for making Pinocchio too American. He failed to persuade the authorities to launch a lawsuit.

After Disney set out to make his film of *Peter Pan,* he became stuck when it came to how Tinker Bell should be depicted. In the end, he decided to model her on the ideal American woman: Marilyn Monroe.

By the time of his death on December 15, 1966, at the age of sixty-five, Disney had won more Oscars (32) than anyone else in history.

Winners of the Cecil B. DeMille Award at the Golden Globes

2004: (awarded in 2005): Robin Williams

2003: Michael Douglas

2002: Gene Hackman

2001: Harrison Ford

2000: Al Pacino

1999: Barbra Streisand

1998: Jack Nicholson

1997: Shirley MacLaine

1996: Dustin Hoffman

1995: Sean Connery

1994: Sophia Loren

1993: Robert Redford

1992: Lauren Bacall

1991: Robert Mitchum

1990: Jack Lemmon

1989: Audrey Hepburn

1988: Doris Day

1987: Clint Eastwood

1986: Anthony Quinn

1985: Barbara Stanwyck

1984: Elizabeth Taylor

1983: Paul Newman

1982: Laurence Olivier

1981: Sidney Poitier

1980: Gene Kelly

1979: Henry Fonda

1978: Lucille Ball

1977: Red Skelton

1976: Walter Mirisch

1975: No Award

1974: Hal B. Wallis

1973: Bette Davis

1972: Samuel Goldwyn

1971: Alfred Hitchcock

1970: Frank Sinatra

1969: Joan Crawford

1968: Gregory Peck

1967: Kirk Douglas

1966: Charlton Heston

1965: John Wayne

1964: James Stewart

1963: Joseph E. Levine

1962: Bob Hope

1961: Judy Garland

1960: Fred Astaire

1959: Bing Crosby

1958: Maurice Chevalier

1957: Buddy Adler

1956: Mervyn LeRoy

1955: Jack L. Warner

1954: Jean Hersholt

1953: Darryl F. Zanuck

1952: Walt Disney

1951: Cecil B. DeMille

Relationships That Started on Film Sets

Tom Cruise and Nicole Kidman (*Days of Thunder*)

Tom Cruise and Penelope Cruz (*Vanilla Sky*)

Meg Ryan and Dennis Quaid (*Innerspace*)

Gwyneth Paltrow and Brad Pitt (*Seven*)

Gwyneth Paltrow and Ben Affleck (*Shakespeare in Love*)

Sadie Frost and Jude Law (*Shopping*)

Ethan Hawke and Uma Thurman (*Gattaca*)

Julia Roberts and Daniel Moder (*The Mexican*)

Jeff Goldblum and Laura Dern (*Jurassic Park*)

William Hurt and Marlee Matlin (*Children of a Lesser God*)

Humphrey Bogart and Lauren Bacall (*To Have and Have Not*)

Warren Beatty and Madonna (*Dick Tracy*)

Laurence Olivier and Vivien Leigh (*Fire Over England*)

Steve McQueen and Ali MacGraw (*The Getaway*)

Paul Hogan and Linda Koslowski (*Crocodile Dundee*)

Richard Burton and Elizabeth Taylor (*Cleopatra*)

Things Robert De Niro Has Done to "Find" His Characters

Raging Bull (1980): For his Oscar-winning role as boxer Jake La Motta, De Niro learned how to box—training with La Motta for six months and breaking the caps on the ex-boxer's teeth. La Motta later said that if De Niro tired of acting, he could earn a living as a boxer. For the film's scenes where his character becomes fat, De Niro gained sixty pounds, which he later shed.

Taxi Driver **(1976):** For this role, De Niro was obliged to *lose* weight—some thirty-five pounds. He also worked as a taxi driver. Once he picked up a fare who, recognizing him, said, "You're the actor, aren't you? Guess it's hard to find steady work."

New York, New York (1977): Most actors, when required to portray musicians, settle for a rough approximation of pretending to play their instruments. Not De Niro. Cast as a saxophonist, he learned to play the saxophone. His playing was still dubbed over by a professional, but his finger placement earned him praise from the experts.

Midnight Run **(1988):** In this comedy-thriller, De Niro played a bounty hunter. To prepare for the role, he went out on the road with a real bounty hunter to see how the job is done. He also learned how to pick a lock for one scene and managed to do it so well that the scene had to be dropped for fear that children would learn the technique from it.

The Deer Hunter (1978): In this film, De Niro played a steel-worker, so he went to live in a steelworking community for a few weeks before starting to film. He also performed his own stunts—including one where he has to jump from a helicopter into the river.

The Godfather, Part II **(1974):** It was for this role, as the young Vito Corleone, that De Niro won his first Oscar. To get into character and play the part with conviction, De Niro learned to speak Sicilian Italian.

The Untouchables (1987): For his brief but brilliant portrayal of Al Capone, De Niro put on weight and inserted plugs into his nose to make him look and sound more like the infamous gangster. He also wore silk underwear bought from the firm that had supplied Capone.

True Confessions **(1981):** One of De Niro's less memorable movies. He played a priest who gets caught up in a murder case involving his policeman brother. Once again, De Niro learned a language for a role—this time, Latin.

A Bronx Tale (1993): This was De Niro's first film as a director, and he was determined that it would be absolutely accurate. He was also playing a part himself—as a bus driver. He trained and then took the New York bus drivers' exam, passing the second time around.

Cape Fear **(1991):** The actor trained for eight months to get his body fat down to just 3 percent for his role as Max Cady.

Accomplished Roller-Bladers

Tom Cruise, Janet Jackson, Dustin Hoffman, Warren Beatty, Peter Gabriel, Emilio Estevez, Nicole Kidman, Robbie Williams, Cher, Daryl Hannah, Bruce Willis, Madonna, Sarah Michelle Gellar, Charisma Carpenter

Avid Anglers

Diana Rigg, Nick Faldo, Robert Redford, Prince Charles, Michael Chang, Tiger Woods, Eric Clapton, Pierce Brosnan, Liam Neeson, Timothy Dalton, Brad Pitt, Carl Hiaasen,  Charlie Sheen, Matthew Modine, Michael Keaton, Peter O'Toole, Roger Federer, Sam Neill

Avid Divers

Richard E. Grant, Chris De Burgh, Gillian Anderson, Nick Carter, Patrick Duffy, Jason Statham (was a professional), Kathleen Quinlan, Tom Hanks, Brooke Shields, Elijah Wood, Heidi Klum, Bill Murray, John Hannah, Josh Brolin, Julianna Margulies, Juliette Binoche, Michael Palin, Natalie Imbruglia, Nick Carter, Anthony Head, Pierce Brosnan, Prince William, Brian May, Ron Howard, Salma Hayek, Sandra Bullock, Val Kilmer, David Hasselhoff

Adept at Needlepoint

Elizabeth Hurley, Sian Phillips, Loretta Swit

Avid Chess Players

Madonna, Guy Ritchie, Sting, Bono, Jude Law, Ewan McGregor, Arnold Schwarzenegger, Jennifer Lopez, Stephen Fry, Greta Scacchi, James Galway, Boris Becker, Al Pacino, Dennis Quaid, Lennox Lewis

Avid Skiers

Jane Asher, Jeremy Irons, Melanie Griffith, Mike Oldfield, Richard Branson, Prince Charles, Roger Moore, Kim Wilde, Don Johnson, Jürgen Prochnow

Avid Waterskiers

Prince William, Minnie Driver

Karate Black Belts

Sharon Stone, Phil Spector, Chuck Norris, Guy Ritchie, John Saxon

Avid Real-Tennis Players

Alan Alda, Martina Navratilova, Prince Edward, Gabriela Sabatini

Fencers

Marcel Marceau, Neil Diamond, Gene Wilder, Mick Fleetwood, Bruce Dickinson, Antonio Banderas, Sylvester Stallone, Catherine Zeta-Jones, Elijah Wood

Adept at Judo

Laetitia Casta (brown belt)

Honor Blackman (brown belt)

David Lee Roth (black belt)

Manuel Noriega (black belt)

Nigel Mansell (black belt)

Vladimir Putin (black belt)

James Cagney (black belt)

Avid Horse Riders

Charisma Carpenter, Kate Moss, Kylie Minogue, Cybill Shepherd, Jane Seymour, Janet Jackson, Lynn Redgrave, Tracey Ullman, Jeremy Irons, Diane Lane, Gisele Bundchen, Laura Linney, LeAnn Rimes, Rachel Hunter

Polo Players

Kenny Jones, Prince Charles, Kerry Packer, Trevor Eve, William Devane, Stacy Keach, Stefanie Powers, Prince William, Ginger Baker, Prince Harry

Good at Do-It-Yourself Projects

Nick Faldo, Harrison Ford (a former carpenter), Courteney Cox, Brad Pitt, Jennifer Lopez, David Beckham, Jeremy Irons, Bill Wyman, Daniel Day-Lewis, Sandra Bullock, Tim Allen

Poker Players

Brad Pitt, David Mamet, Bill Gates, Martin Amis, Matt Damon, Ben Affleck, David Schwimmer, Mimi Rogers, Tobey Maguire, Jennifer Aniston, James Woods, Leonardo DiCaprio, Stephen Fry, Ricky Gervais, Joan Collins, Vinnie Jones, Salman Rushdie

Avid Knitters

Julia Roberts, Cameron Diaz, Russell Crowe, Uma Thurman, Winona Ryder, Goldie Hawn, Naomi Campbell, Julianne Moore, David Duchovny, Kate Beckinsale, Bridget Fonda, Sandra Bullock, Anjelica Huston, Kate Moss, David Arquette, Geri Halliwell, Madonna, Iman, Hilary Swank, Daryl Hannah, Sarah Jessica Parker

Cartoonists/Caricaturists

David Beckham, Moby, Patricia Cornwell, Will Self, George Clooney

Religion

Psalm 117 ("O praise the LORD, all ye nations: praise him, all ye people. For his merciful kindness is great toward us: and the truth of the LORD endureth for ever. Praise ye the LORD") is the shortest chapter in the Bible: it is also the center chapter in the Bible. However, the middle two *verses* of the Bible are in Psalm 118.

Forty-nine different kinds of food are mentioned in the Bible.

The religion of the Todas people of southern India forbids them to cross any kind of bridge.

On July 1, 2003, the First Baptist Church in Forest, Ohio, was struck by lightning just as the visiting evangelist was telling the congregation that "God's voice often sounds like thunder."

Some saints in the Middle Ages kept themselves dirty because they thought it would bring them closer to God.

During the First Crusade, a band of religious hysterics marched behind a goose they believed was filled with the Holy Spirit.

Belief in the existence of vacuums used to be punishable by death under church law.

Playing music containing augmented-fourth chords was avoided because it was thought to invoke the devil.

There's a temple in Sri Lanka dedicated to a tooth of the Buddha.

In 1654, Bishop Ussher of Ireland, having analyzed all the "begats" in Genesis, concluded that planet Earth had been created at 9:00 A.M. on October 26, 4004 B.C., a Thursday.

St. John was the only one of the twelve apostles to die a natural death.

Most of the villains in the Bible have red hair.

David is the most common name in the Bible. Jesus is second.

Pope Paul IV was so outraged when he saw the naked bodies on the ceiling of the Sistine Chapel that he ordered Michelangelo to paint garments on them.

The term "devil's advocate" comes from the Roman Catholic Church. When someone was being considered for sainthood, a devil's advocate was appointed to give an alternative view.

The word "Sunday" is not in the Bible.

219

A Guide to Different Religions

Taoism: Shit happens.

Zen: What is the sound of shit happening?

Hinduism: This shit's happened before.

Buddhism: If shit happens, it isn't really shit.

Islam: If shit happens, it's the will of Allah.

Protestantism: Shit happens because we don't work hard enough.

Catholicism: Shit happens because we are bad.

Christian Fundamentalism: Shit happens because the Bible says so.

Jehovah's Witnesses: Knock, knock. "Shit happens."

Judaism: Why does shit always happen to us?

Agnosticism: We don't know shit.

Atheism: No shit.

Hare Krishna: Shit happens—rama lama ding dong.

Rastafarianism: Let's smoke this shit.

Scientologists

Tom Cruise, Chick Corea, John Travolta, Priscilla Presley, Kirstie Alley, Isaac Hayes, Anne Archer, Kelly Preston, Mimi Rogers, Sharon Stone, Beck

Buddhists

Uma Thurman, Stephanie Beacham, Keanu Reeves, Cindy Crawford, Susan Sarandon, Sandie Shaw, Woody Harrelson, Tina Turner, Courtney Love, Harrison Ford, Richard Gere, Koo Stark, Oliver Stone, Pamela Stephenson, Claudia Schiffer, Annie Lennox, Jim Carrey, Björk

Born Roman Catholics

Christina Aguilera, Farrah Fawcett, Eddie Van Halen, Nick Nolte, Rosie O'Donnell, Regis Philbin, Celine Dion, Rupert Everett, Ben Affleck, Jean-Claude Van Damme, Antonio Banderas, Martin Scorsese, Nicolas Cage, Camille Paglia, Brigitte Bardot, Sylvester Stallone, Pierce Brosnan, Pelé, Lara Flynn Boyle, Paul McCartney, Catherine Deneuve, Faye Dunaway, Mel Gibson, Martin Sheen, Liam Neeson, Madonna, Cyndi Lauper, Arnold Schwarzenegger, Brooke Shields, Sean Penn, Bianca Jagger, Al Pacino, Robert De Niro, John McEnroe, Anne Bancroft, Bill Murray, Luciano Pavarotti, Sophia Loren, Alanis Morissette, Natalie

Imbruglia, Heather Graham, Tommy Hilfiger, Claudia Schiffer, Gabriel Byrne, Danny DeVito, Jim Carrey, Martin Short, Joe Pesci, Catherine Zeta-Jones, Jennifer Lopez, Salma Hayek, John Cusack, Haley Joel Osment, Matt Dillon, Rachel Hunter, Kelsey Grammer, Lucy Lawless, Chris O'Donnell, Gwen Stefani, Alyssa Milano, Noel and Liam Gallagher, Patsy Kensit, Brendan Fraser, Juliette Binoche, Ray Liotta, Mira Sorvino, Elvis Costello, Mary Tyler Moore, Mia Farrow, Alan Alda, Meg Ryan, Melissa Joan Hart, Tom Clancy, Dan Aykroyd, Aidan Quinn, Jack Nicholson, Denise Richards, J. D. Salinger, Charlotte Church, Minnie Driver, Joey Fatone, Lea Salonga, Jon Bon Jovi, Pete Postlethwaite, Judy Davis, Victoria Principal, Mandy Moore, Michael Crawford, Christy Turlington, Gloria Estefan, Axl Rose, Julian Clary, Jodie Foster, Ray Liotta, Anna Nicole Smith, Diego Maradona, Belinda Carlisle, Pat Cash, Goran Ivanisevic, Franz Beckenbauer, Elijah Wood, Bruce Springsteen, Delia Smith, Chris De Burgh, Whoopi Goldberg, Johnny Vaughan

Born Jewish

Alicia Silverstone, Gwyneth Paltrow, David Copperfield, William Shatner, Randy Newman, Yasmine Bleeth, Ben Stiller, Jerry Seinfeld, Natalie Portman, Sarah Jessica

Parker, Joel Stransky, Gary Kasparov, Calvin Klein, Debra Winger, Geraldo Rivera, David Blaine, Rodney Dangerfield, Artie Shaw, Elizabeth Taylor (convert), Harvey Keitel, Leonard Nimoy, Tony Curtis, Gene Simmons, Barry Manilow, Hank Azaria, Barbra Streisand, Neil Diamond, Manfred Mann, Leonard Cohen, Adam Sandler, Vidal Sassoon, Herb Alpert, Lauren Bacall, Dyan Cannon, Peter Green, Cyd Charisse, Gloria Steinem, Jerry Springer, Marcel Marceau, Carly Simon, Roman Polanski, Phil Spector, Mel Tormé, Jody Scheckter, Larry King, Howard Stern, Neil Sedaka, Norman Mailer, James Caan, Lou Reed, Paul Simon, Art Garfunkel, Bette Midler, Billy Crystal, Billy Joel, Henry Winkler, Goldie Hawn, Rachel Stevens, Winona Ryder, Carole King, Bob Dylan, Noah Wyle, Burt Bacharach, Helen Reddy, Ruth Prawer Jhabvala, Alicia Markova, Barbara Walters

Born Jehovah's Witnesses

Hank B. Marvin, Venus and Serena Williams, the Jacksons (although Michael joined the Nation of Islam in December 2003), Prince, Geri Halliwell (raised as one by her mother), Dwight Eisenhower (raised as one), Roy Harper, Mickey Spillane, Viv Nicholson

223

Born Lutherans

Loni Anderson, Beau Bridges, Jeff Bridges, David Hasselhoff, William Hurt, William H. Macy, Ann-Margret, David Soul, Sally Struthers, Liv Ullmann, Bruce Willis, Gary Larson, Theodore Geisel (aka Dr. Seuss), Elke Sommer, Dana Carvey, Johann Sebastian Bach, John Woo, Norman Schwarzkopf, Edwin Meese, William Rehnquist, Kris Kristofferson, Lyle Lovett, John Mellencamp, Dag Hammarskjöld, Søren Kierkegaard, Dr. Albert Schweitzer, Dietrich Bonhoeffer, Martin Niemoeller, Lou Gehrig, Andy North, Duffy Waldorf, Garrison Keillor

Born Mormons

Rick Schroeder, Matthew Modine, Robert Walker, the Osmonds, Gladys Knight, Randy Bachman

Born Quakers

Judi Dench, Richard Nixon, James Michener, Herbert Hoover, David Lean, Cheryl Tiegs, Bradley Whitford

Born Baptists

Britney Spears, John Bunyan, Warren G. Harding, Harry S. Truman, Bill Clinton, Clarence Thomas, Newt Gingrich, Al Gore, Martin Luther King, Jesse Jackson, Payne Stewart, Jonathan Edwards, Glen Campbell, Donna Summer, Jessica Simpson, Otis Redding, Aretha Franklin, John Grisham, Chuck Norris, Billy Graham

Converted to Islam

Michael Jackson, Muhammad Ali, Mike Tyson, Malcolm X, Gérard Depardieu (although he later converted back to Christianity), Art Blakey, Cat Stevens

Christian Scientists

Ginger Rogers, Jim Henson, H. R. Haldeman, Doris Day, Carol Channing, Lady Nancy Astor, Robert Duvall, Joan Crawford, Val Kilmer

N.B.: The parents of V. S. Pritchett, Elizabeth Taylor, Jean Harlow, Ellen DeGeneres and Dudley Moore were all Christian Scientists.

Born-Again Christians

Charlene Tilton, Andre Agassi, Samantha Fox, Cuba Gooding Jr., Jane Russell, Stephen Baldwin, Jane Fonda, Jo Ann Pflug

Into Kabbalah

Madonna, Guy Ritchie, Demi Moore, Elton John, Mick Jagger, Jeff Goldblum, Naomi Campbell, Elizabeth Taylor, Barbra Streisand, Courtney Love

Considered Becoming Priests

Joseph Stalin, Ben Vereen, Charles Darwin, Mike McShane, Bob Guccione, Bernhard Langer, Gabriel Byrne, Roberto Benigni, Tom Cruise (at age fourteen, he enrolled in a seminary but dropped out after a year), John Woo, Pete Postlethwaite

Considered Becoming Rabbis

Gene Simmons, Leonard Bernstein

N.B.: Jackie Mason *was* a rabbi

Might Have Become Nuns

Heather Graham (Her parents had ambitions for her to become one.)

Kristin Scott Thomas (At age sixteen, she enrolled in a convent school with a view to becoming a nun.)

Cher ("There was a time when I nearly became a nun myself, but it didn't last long.")

Zoë Wanamaker ("Despite being born Jewish . . . ")

Francesca Annis (She wanted to be a nun.)

Agnostics

Uma Thurman, Michael Palin, David Bowie, Stephen Hawking, Carrie Fisher, James Taylor, Sean Penn, Larry King, Roman Polanski, Matt Groening, Al Stewart

Atheists

Bill Gates, Woody Allen, Richard Branson, Arthur C. Clarke, Amanda Donohoe, Patrick Duffy, Larry Flynt, Dario Fo, Jodie Foster, Debbie Harry, Margot Kidder, David Cronenberg, Brian Eno, John Fowles, Kinky Friedman, Janeane Garofalo, Björk, John Carpenter, Fidel Castro, Harvey Fierstein, Angelina Jolie, Neil Jordan, John Malkovich, Barry Manilow, Camille Paglia, Steven Soderbergh, Gore Vidal, Nick Mason, Ian McKellen, Terry Pratchett, Howard Stern, Michael Stipe, Tom Lehrer, Mike Leigh, Alexander McQueen, Arthur Miller, Randy Newman, Jack Nicholson, James Randi, Donald Sutherland

Flags

The state flag of Alaska was designed by a thirteen-year-old boy.

Egypt, Dominica, Mexico, Fiji, Zambia and Kiribati all have birds on their flags.

Texas is the only U.S. state allowed to fly its state flag at the same height as the U.S. flag.

The Dominican Republic has the only national flag with a Bible on it.

Cyprus has its outline on its flag.

Nepal is the only country without a rectangular flag.

Libya has the only flag that's one color (green) with nothing else on it.

Banished Words

Since 1976, Lake Superior State University in Michigan has been publishing its annual list of "Words Banished from the Queen's English for Mis-use, Over-use and General Uselessness."

THE 2005 LIST

BLUE STATES/RED STATES—Who's who, anyway? A good map has more than two colors.

FLIP-FLOP / FLIP-FLOPPER / FLIP-FLOPPING—They belong at the beach, not in a political dialogue.

BATTLEGROUND STATE—During an election, every state is a battleground.

". . . AND I APPROVE THIS MESSAGE"—Received the most nominations of the words and phrases that came out of the presidential election. From political ads to auto parts . . .

POCKETS OF RESISTANCE—Sounds like someone having trouble pulling their hands out of their pants pockets.

IMPROVISED EXPLOSIVE DEVICE—As opposed to what used to be referred to as a bomb or mine.

ENEMY COMBATANT—Makes no sense. Do we have friendly combatants? Neutral combatants? Or how about enemy bystanders? If they are your enemy, just say so.

CARBS—Low carbs, high carbs, no carbs, carb-friendly . . . Meant "carburetor" in a previous life. Needs to be purged from our system.

YOU'RE FIRED!—". . . and the little hand movement, too!" One nominator suggested that to say it would soon constitute a trademark infringement.

ÜBER—Nominated by many over the past few years. . . . Everything that is big, amazing, unique is described as über.

"IZZLE"-SPEAK—By far, the abomination that received the most nominations. Some sort of Rap-Latin suffix, as in "fa'shizzle," which means "for sure."

WARDROBE MALFUNCTION—Janet Jackson's bodice did not "malfunction." Justin Timberlake pulled too much and too far.

BLOG—And its variations, including blogger, blogged, blogging, blogosphere. Many who nominated it were unsure of the meaning. Sounds like something your mother would slap you for saying.

WEBINAR—"Seminar on the Web."

ZERO PERCENT APR FINANCING—Sending a dollar to do a nickel's worth of work.

SAFE AND EFFECTIVE—Try the new, clinically proven, safe and effective wonder drug you never knew you needed. . . . Safe and effective should not be a selling point, it should be an FDA requirement!

ERECTILE DYSFUNCTION—Do we need to hear about it daily on TV and radio, even on race cars?

JOURNEY—Every single person on every reality show comments on how amazing the "journey" was. Since when does dating a dozen nerds over a six-week span or conniving to win a million dollars over fifteen other people qualify as a "journey"?

BODY WASH—Also known as "soap."

SALE EVENT—Year-end sales are now "sales events." Now most have shortened it to "event." Does the sale exist any longer?

ALL NEW—Referring to television shows. . . . Of course it's all new. Why can't they just say "new"?

AND MORE!—The merchant's way of giving you something "value added."

231

Some of the Banished Words from 1976–2004 in Alphabetical Order

24/7 2000

Academically fragile 2001

Academically ineligible 1993

Active possibility 1977

Actual facts 1991

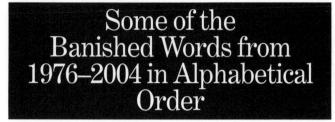

Adults over twenty-one 1988

Afterfeel 1987

Alcohol-related drunk driving 1989

All except 1990

All-time record 1982

Almost exactly 1990

Alternative lifestyle 1988

Always consistent 1994

Armed and dangerous 1996

Armed gunman 1993

As if 1997

As per 2003

At risk 2000

At this point in time 1976

Awesome 1984

Baby boomers 1989

Ballpark figure 1980

Bare naked 1985

Basically 1984, 1986, 1993

Been there, done that. 1996

Begs the question 2001

Best-kept secret 1990

Big time 1992

Bill Clinton and Monica Lewinsky 1999

The bottom line 1979, 1992

Brainstorm/brainstorming 2002

"Bring them to justice" or "Bring the evildoers to justice." 2002

Build-down 1984

(The) bullet went all the way through the body. 1983

By and large 1987

Campaign rhetoric 1981

233

Carjacking 2002

Cautiously optimistic 1992

Ceremonialization 1984

Chad 2001

Chill out 1980

Classic 1982, 1989

Clearly ambiguous 1994

Close proximity 1990

Close to everything 1991

Closure 1996

Community 1992

Completely empty 1993

Conceptualize 1983

Connect or hook up 1992

Consumer confidence 1995

Conventional wisdom 1993

Courtesy call 1999

Cult classic 1989

Cutting edge 1988

Cyber 1996

Dead meat 1991

Dead serious 1994

Definite possibilities 1993

Deinstall 1987

Delay due to an earlier accident 2002

Deplane 1981

Docudrama 1989

Doing the —— thing 1997

Don't (even) go there. 1997

Done deal 1996

Done in good taste 1986

Dot.com 2001

Downsizing 1993

Down time 1997

Drug czar 1990

Dude 2001

Dysfunctional 1994

"Ɛ"-anything 2000

Each and every one of you 1996

Eh 1979

Enclosed please find 1985, 1989

End result 1991

Exact same 1981, 1990

Extreme 2003

Faith-based 2002

False pretenses 1991

Family values 1995

Filmed before a live studio audience 1983, 1987, 1990

Final destination 2001

First time ever 1982, 1983

Forced relaxation 1989

Foreign imports 1987

Foreseeable future 2002

Free gift 1988

Fresh frozen 1989

Friendly fire 2002

Gathered together 1994

Get a life 1997

Giving 110 percent 1998

Grass roots 1993

Gridlock 1993

Gun control 1994

Gut feeling 1983

Handcrafted latte 2004

Hands-on participatory experience 1987

Happy camper 1993

Have a good one! 2001

Having said that 2003

He/she 1994

The health-care delivery system/industry 1987

Hello!? 1999

High-tech 1984

(The) honest truth 1991

Hopefully 1978

Humanitarian 1995

I feel your pain. 1995

I know where I'm coming from. 1978

(But) I don't know where you're coming from. 1978

I see what you are saying. 1992

If —, then the terrorists win. 2002

I'm 150 percent behind you. 1995

I'm like 1997

I'm talkin — here. 1987

In my humble opinion 1992

In terms of 1982

In the public interest 1980

In the wake of 2002

In your face 1993

Incentivize, -izing, -ized 1983

Information superhighway 1995

Infotainment 1986, 1989

Input 1976

Interface 1980

Issues 2000

It's the pits. 1980

Jumbo shrimp 1995

Large-size petites 1990

Let's do lunch. 1986

Level playing field 1992

To liaison with 1982

Like (*see also* I'm like) 1997

Like I said 1986

Listen up. 1983

Living in poverty 1988

Longer hours 1991

Managing terrorism 1989

Mandate 1985

Manual recount by hand 2001

Material breach 2003

Mc(anything) 1986

Mean-spirited 1995

Meaningful dialogue 1976

Metrosexual 2004

Millennium 2000

Mission statement 1996

Mopping-up operation 1991

Moral majority 1981

More importantly 1992

More than happy 1994

The more you buy, the more you save. 1990

Most complete 1993

Mother of all —— 1994

Multitasking 1997

Must-see TV 2003

Near miss 1985

Negative growth 2001

Neonatal unit 1987

Networking 1988

New innovation 1990

New kid on the street/block 1984

Nine/eleven (9/11) 2002

No-brainer 2002

No problem 1980

Not 1993

Now, more than ever 2003

On a —— basis 1991

On a roll 1984, 1988

On the ground 2003

Ongoing 1984, 1986, 1993

Online 1996

Outsourcing 1997

Overview 1992

Parenting skills 1991

Past history 1981

Past experience 1994

The patient did not fulfill his wellness potential. 1987

Paying my dues 1981

Peacekeeping force 1996

—— **percent pure** 1995

Peel-and-eat shrimp 2003

Perfectly candid 1977

Perimeters/parameters 1979

Political reality 1983

Political strongman 1990

Politically correct 1994

Postconsumer products 1995

Postmodern 1984

Potential hazard 1987

Preboard 1980

Preplan 1983

Prequel 1985

Preventive maintenance 1987

Prioritize 1978

Proactive 1991, 1993

Process 1978

Pushing the envelope 1995

Quality of life 2000

Quality time 1985

241

The race card 1996

Read my lips 1989

Reaffirm 1988

Reaganomics 1983

Reality TV 2002

Really 1979

The reason is because 1985

Refusenik 1988

Rename it something else. 2002

Reverse discrimination 2003

Road rage 2000

Rocket scientist 1991

Rush hour 1990

Safe haven 1993

Safe sex 1988

Same difference 1987

Sanction 1992

Scenario 1976

Scenario 1991

Sea change 2000

Secluded privacy 1988

Senseless murder 1984

Serves no useful purpose 1981

Signage 1987

Situation 1978

Sketchy details 1994

Slight glitch 1995

Smoking gun 2004

So 1999

Somewhere down the road 1979

Sound bite 1989

Speaks to 2001

Spearhead 1994

Spin doctor 1989

State of the art 1983

Step up / step it up 1999

Stun 1999

Sucks 1995

Supermarket fresh 1989

Superstar 1984

Surely if we can send a man to the moon, we can ——. 1980

Surgical strike 2002

243

Surrounding environs 1992

Sworn affidavit 2002

Synergy 2002

A tad 1987

Talk to the hand 1998

Take it to the next level. 1998

Target audience 1995

Task 1988

That said 2003

There you go. 1987

Thinking outside the box 2000

Time frame 1980

To be perfectly honest with you 1992

To die for 1995

Too right 1989

Total capacity of this room limited to 100 persons. 1989

Totally unique 2002

Touch base 1996

Track record 1991

Trained professional 1993

Turned up missing 1987

Two twins 1991

Undisclosed, secret location 2003

Unplugged 1996

Unprecedented new 2002

Unrequested leave of absence 1991

Untimely death 2003

Up front 1992

Up to speed 1985

Use only as directed. 1988

User-friendly 1984

Utilize 1987

Vast majority 1995

Very unique 1983, 2002

Viable 1976

Viable alternative 1979, 1992

Victimless crime 1993

Virtual reality 1996

Vison statement 1996

Visual view 1986

Visually eyeball the runway 1985

Void where prohibited 1988

Wake-up call 2000

We must focus our attention. 1983

Weapons of mass destruction 2003

Went ballistic 1993

What are you into? 1979

Whatever 1997

Whatsup? 1998

Win-win 1993

Window of opportunity 1991

Working mother 1983

World-class 1982, 1993

Y2K 1999

Yadda, yadda, yadda 1998

Yo 1990

You go, girl. 1997

You got it. 1985

You'd better believe 1978

Your call is very important to us. 1996

Yuppie 1986

Zero percent increase 1991

Lennon and McCartney Songs Never Released by the Beatles (apart from on the anthologies)

"Bad to Me" (Billy J. Kramer and the Dakotas)

"Nobody I Know" (Peter and Gordon)

"Like Dreamers Do" (The Applejacks)

"Tip of My Tongue" (Tommy Quickly)

"Step Inside Love" (Cilla Black)

"That Means a Lot" (P. J. Proby)

"A World Without Love" (Peter and Gordon)

"I'm in Love" (The Fourmost)

"One and One Is Two" (The Strangers with Mike Shannon)

"It's for You" (Cilla Black)

"Hello Little Girl" (The Fourmost)

"I'll Keep You Satisfied" (Billy J. Kramer and the Dakotas)

Covers of Beatles Songs

"Got to Get You into My Life" (Joe Pesci)

"Something" (Telly Savalas)

"Lucy in the Sky with Diamonds" (William Shatner)

"I Am the Walrus" (Jim Carrey)

"Love Me Do" (The Brady Bunch)

"A Hard Day's Night" (Peter Sellers)

"Blackbird" (Kevin Spacey)

"I Want You (She's So Heavy)" (Donald Pleasence)

"We Can Work It Out" (George Burns)

"Come Together" (Robin Williams)

"All My Loving" (Alvin and the Chipmunks)

"Yellow Submarine" (Milton Berle)

Beatles Songs and Their Working Titles

"Hello Goodbye"—Hello Hello

"A Day in the Life"—In the Life Of

"Yesterday"—Scrambled Eggs

"It's Only Love"—That's a Nice Hat

"Think for Yourself"—Won't Be There with You

 **"Flying"**—Aerial Tour Instrumental

"Eleanor Rigby"—Miss Daisy Hawkins

"Thank You Girl"—Thank You Little Girl

"Love You To"—Granny Smith

"I Saw Her Standing There"—Seventeen

Acts Signed to Apple Records

James Taylor, Hot Chocolate, Ronnie Spector, Billy Preston

Songs About the Beatles

"All I Want for Christmas Is a Beatle" (Dora Bryan): The most successful Beatles tribute record in the U.K.—it reached #20 in 1963.

"We Love You Beatles" (The Carefrees): The most successful Beatles tribute song in the U.S.—it reached #39 in 1964.

"My Girlfriend Wrote a Letter to the Beatles" (The Four Preps): And guess what? They didn't write back.

249

"I Wanna Be a Beatle" (Gene Cornish and the Unbeatables): Soon after recording this, they changed their name to the Young Rascals (and had hits including "Groovin'").

"Ringo, I Love You" (Bonnie Jo Mason): Bonnie Jo Mason was a pseudonym for Cher.

"A Beatle I Want to Be" (Sonny Curtis): Sonny was one of Buddy Holly's Crickets—and the Fab Four had named themselves after the Crickets.

"I Hate the Beatles" (Allan Sherman): Sherman was an American humorous singer whose only British hit was "Hello Muddah, Hello Faddah."

"Get Back Beatles" (Gerard Kenny): Kenny later wrote the song "New York, New York" (not the Sinatra one, but the one that goes "New York, New York, so nice they named it twice").

"I'm Better Than the Beatles" (Brad Berwick and the Bugs): History would suggest otherwise. . . .

"The Beatles' Barber" (Scott Douglas): About a man who has been put out of work because the Fabs never have their mop tops cut. Or something.

"Ringo for President" (Rolf Harris): American presidents have to be American—which might explain why the song bombed.

Singers Who Refer to Themselves by Name in Songs

"The Universal" (The Small Faces—Steve Marriott on vocals, 1968)

"I Feel for You" (Chaka Khan, 1984)

"Blue Motel Room" (Joni Mitchell, 1976)

"My Name Is Prince" (Prince, 1992)

"Sweet Baby James" (James Taylor, 1970)

"Strong Persuader" (Robert Cray, 1986)

"Creeque Alley" (The Mamas and the Papas—Mama Cass Elliot on vocals, 1967)

"The Mind of Love" (k. d. lang, 1992)

"Float On" (The Floaters—all of them individually, 1977)

"Wannabe" (The Spice Girls—all of them individually, 1996)

"Brooklyn Roads" (Neil Diamond, 1976)

Duets

Catherine Zeta-Jones and David Essex on "True Love Ways," 1994

Rock Hudson and Rod McKuen on "Love of the Common Celebrities," 1970

Peter Sellers and Sophia Loren on "Goodness Gracious Me," 1959

Don Johnson and Barbra Streisand on "Till I Loved You" (Love Theme from *Goya*), 1988

Beavis, Butt-Head and Cher on "I Got You Babe," 1994

Bruce Willis and the Pointer Sisters on "Respect Yourself," 1987

Ewan McGregor and Nicole Kidman on "Come What May," 2001

Michael J. Fox and Joan Jett on "Light of Day," 1986

Victoria Principal and Andy Gibb on "All I Have to Do Is Dream," 1981

Joan Collins and Bing Crosby on "Let's Not Be Sensible," 1962

Madeline Kahn and Frankie Laine on "Blazing Saddles," in 1973

Alain Delon and Shirley Bassey on the album *Shirley Bassey & Alain Delon* 1984

People Immortalized in Song Titles

Smokey Robinson—"When Smokey Sings" (ABC, 1987)

Spencer Tracy—"He Looks Like Spencer Tracy Now" (Deacon Blue, 1988)

Grigory Rasputin—"Rasputin" (Boney M, 1978)

Buddy Holly—"I Feel Like Buddy Holly" (Alvin Stardust, 1984)

Otis Redding—"Ode to Otis Redding" (Mark Johnson, 1968)

Elvis Presley—"Elvis Presley and America" (U2, 1984)

Dolly Parton—"Dolly Parton's Guitar" (Lee Hazlewood, 1977)

Jackie Wilson—"Jackie Wilson Said" (Van Morrison, 1972)

Bo Diddley—"The Story of Bo Diddley" (The Animals, 1964)

Hank Williams—"The Night Hank Williams Came to Town" (Johnny Cash, 1986)

Michael Caine—"Michael Caine" (Madness, 1984)

Benito Mussolini—"Do the Mussolini" (Cabaret Voltaire, 1978)

Robert De Niro—"Robert De Niro's Waiting"
(Bananarama, 1984)

Bonnie Parker and Clyde Barrow—"Ballad of Bonnie and Clyde"
(Georgie Fame, 1967)

Sean Penn—"Sean Penn Blues" (Lloyd Cole and the
Commotions, 1987)

Kaiser Wilhelm II—"I Was Kaiser Bill's Batman"
(Whistling Jack Smith, 1967)

Aretha Franklin—"Aretha, Sing One for Me" (George
Jackson, 1971)

Michael Jackson—"Dear Michael" (Kim Fields, 1984)

Lee Remick—"Lee Remick" (The Go-Betweens, 1978)

Bette Davis—"Bette Davis Eyes" (Kim Carnes, 1981)

John Wayne—"John Wayne Is Big Leggy" (Haysi Fantayzee,
1982)

Linda Evans—"Linda Evans" (The Walkabouts, 1987)

Vincent van Gogh—"Vincent" (Don McLean, 1972)

Andy Warhol—"Andy Warhol" (David Bowie,
1971)

Jim Reeves—"Tribute to Jim Reeves" (Larry
Cunningham, 1964)

Marvin Gaye—"Marvin" (Edwin
Starr, 1984)

Pure Trivia, V

It is physically impossible for pigs to look up into the sky.

The man who invented FM radio was Edwin Armstrong. The first men to use FM radio to communicate with Earth from the Moon's surface were Edwin "Buzz" Aldrin and Neil Armstrong.

Iceland consumes more Coca-Cola per capita than any other nation.

Camel-hair brushes are made from squirrel hair.

Genghis Khan's original name was Temujin. He started out as a goatherd.

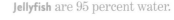

Jellyfish are 95 percent water.

The Lazy Susan is named after Thomas Edison's daughter. He invented it to impress a gathering of industrialists and inventors.

Mickey Mouse's ears are always turned to the front, no matter which direction his nose is pointing.

Cows give more milk when they listen to music.

Mozart never went to school.

Nanotechnology has produced a guitar no bigger than a blood cell. The guitar, 10 micrometers long, has strings which can be strummed.

On March 29, 1848, Niagara Falls stopped flowing for thirty hours because of an ice jam blocking the Niagara river.

To see a rainbow, you must have your back to the sun.

Rubber bands last longer when refrigerated.

South Africa used to have two official languages. Now it has eleven.

Seven percent of the entire Irish barley crop goes into the making of Guinness.

The national anthem of Greece is 158 verses long.

The original Guinness Brewery in Dublin has a six-thousand-year lease.

Since 1896, the beginning of the modern Olympics, only Greece and Australia have participated in every games.

Thomas Edison, the inventor of the lightbulb, was afraid of the dark.

The Albanian language, one of Europe's oldest, isn't derived from any other language.

Abraham Lincoln's Gettysburg Address was just 267 words long.

Men of the Walibri tribe of central Australia greet each other by shaking each other's penis instead of each other's hand.

Huge wine jugs were often used by the ancient Greeks as coffins.

Wade Morrison, the inventor of Dr Pepper, named the drink after Dr. Charles Pepper, who had given him his first job.

Bugs Bunny was originally called "Happy Rabbit."

Mao Tse-tung never brushed his teeth, but washed his mouth with tea instead.

The average four-year-old child asks over 400 questions a day.

The oldest living thing in the world is a creosote bush in south-western California, which is more than 11,000 years old.

The expression "second string," meaning replacement or backup, comes from the Middle Ages. An archer always carried a second string in case the one on his bow broke.

Counting how many times a cricket chirps in 15 seconds and then adding 40 to that number will tell you roughly what the outside temperature is in Fahrenheit.

Studies indicate that weight lifters working out in blue gyms can handle heavier weights.

Pepper was sold in individual grains during Elizabethan times.

The average ratio of yellow kernels to white kernels in a bag of popcorn is 9:1.

One bale of cotton will yield 215 pairs of jeans.

All the Winners of the Grammy for Best New Artist

2004 (awarded in 2005): Maroon 5

2003: Evanescence

2002: Norah Jones

2001: Alicia Keys

2000: Shelby Lynne

1999: Christina Aguilera

1998: Lauryn Hill

1997: Paula Cole

1996: LeAnn Rimes

1995: Hootie & the Blowfish

1994: Sheryl Crow

1993: Toni Braxton

1992: Arrested Development

1991: Marc Cohn

1990: Mariah Carey

1989: Awarded to Milli Vanilli, but later withdrawn

1988: Tracy Chapman

1987: Jody Watley

1986: Bruce Hornsby and the Range

1985: Sade

1984: Cyndi Lauper

1983: Culture Club

1982: Men at Work

1981: Sheena Easton

1980: Christopher Cross

1979: Rickie Lee Jones

1978: A Taste of Honey

1977: Debby Boone

1976: Starland Vocal Band

1975: Natalie Cole

1974: Marvin Hamlisch

1973: Bette Midler

1972: America

1971: Carly Simon

1970: The Carpenters

1969: Crosby Stills & Nash

1968: Jose Feliciano

1967: Bobbie Gentry

1966: No award

1965: Tom Jones

1964: The Beatles

1963: The Swingle Sisters

1962: Robert Goulet

1961: Peter Nero

1960: Bob Newhart

1959: Bobby Darin

Appeared in Music Videos

Jennifer Lopez—"That's the Way Love Goes" by Janet Jackson

Elijah Wood—"Ridiculous Thought" by the Cranberries

Wesley Snipes—"Bad" by Michael Jackson

Ian McKellen—"Heart" by the Pet Shop Boys

Naomi Campbell—"I'll Tumble for Ya" by Culture Club

Chevy Chase—"You Can Call Me Al" by Paul Simon

Mike Tyson—"Bad Boy 4 Life" by Puff Daddy

Donald Sutherland—"Cloudbusting" by Kate Bush

Claudia Schiffer—"Uptown Girl" by Westlife

Kirsten Dunst—"I Knew I Loved You" by Savage Garden

Carmen Electra—"We Are All Made of Stars" by Moby

Danny DeVito—"When the Going Gets Tough" by Billy Ocean

Michelle Pfeiffer—"Gangsta's Paradise" by Coolio (she was also in the horn section for B. B. King's "In the Midnight Hour")

Angelina Jolie—"Rock & Roll Dreams Come Through" by Meat Loaf

George Clooney—"She's Just Killin' Me" by ZZ Top

Daryl Hannah—"Feel" by Robbie Williams

Johnny Depp—"Into the Wide Great Open" by Tom Petty

A Guide to ABBA

In the Bible, *abba*, meaning "father," is used to refer to God. In Sweden, Abba is the name of a fish-canning company.

ABBA made their name by winning the 1974 Eurovision Song Contest with "Waterloo," but they were originally going to do a song called "Hasta Mañana," which featured a lead vocal by Agnetha. In the end, they chose "Waterloo" because it was a group song.

ABBA's former name was "Festfolk." It was under this name that the foursome of Björn, Benny, Agnetha and Anni-Frid made their debut in a Gothenberg restaurant in November 1970.

"Fernando" is the biggest-selling single in Australian chart history—having spent 15 weeks at #1 there. It was also featured, along with other ABBA songs, in the Australian film *Muriel's Wedding.*

ABBA's only #1 single in the United States is "Dancing Queen," although they have had other Top 10 hits—starting with "Waterloo," which was the first Eurovision Song Contest song to reach the U.S. Top 10.

Benny owns a riding stable and has named some of his horses after guitars—for example, "Burns," "Gretch" and "Rickenbacker."

Lasse Hallström (*Cider House Rules, Chocolat*) directed almost every one of ABBA's music videos—as well as *ABBA: The Movie.*

ABBA's distinctive vocal-harmony sound was invented by their engineer, Michael B. Tretow, who, inspired by Phil Spector, found a way to alter the speed slightly between overdubs.

Drummers

Madonna (The Breakfast Club)

Joe Cocker (The Cavaliers)

Frank Zappa (The Black-outs)

Billy Bob Thornton (Tres Hombres, a ZZ Top cover band)

Mel Brooks (various bands)

Peter Gabriel (various bands)

Peter Sellers (in dance bands)

April Fools' Day Pranks

In 1992, a joker fitted a huge sign onto the roof of the stand at the Hollywood Park racetrack, reading WELCOME TO CHICAGO. This was visible to all passengers on flights coming into Los Angeles and caused no little consternation.

Probably the most famous British April Fools' Day prank was the Spaghetti Harvest on BBC TV's *Panorama* in 1957. Its host was the venerable Richard Dimbleby, definitely *not* a prankster, and millions of people were taken in when he told them about the spaghetti harvest and showed them the spaghetti "growing" and being "dried" in the sun.

In 1994, the Mars candy company took out full-page advertisements in British newspapers announcing their "New Biggest Ever Mars Bar." The "Emperor"-size Mars Bar was thirty-two pounds of "thick chocolate, glucose and milk." It was "on sale" for only one day. April 1.

In 1979, London's Capital Radio announced that because of all the constant changing between British Summertime and Greenwich Mean Time, we had gained an extra forty-eight hours, which would have to be lost by the cancellation of April 5 and April 12. Listeners phoned in wondering what would happen to birthdays, anniversaries and other such things.

Not to be outdone, in 1980 the BBC World Service told its listeners that Big Ben's clockface would be replaced by a digital face. Since the World Service is treated with a lot of reverence, many people were taken in.

In 1983, the German car firm BMW ran a full-page advertisement for "the first open-top car to keep out the rain even when it's stationary" (supposedly something to do with "artificial airstreams"). Other years have produced gems such as "A BMW you need never wash again," "WARNING: are you driving a genuine BMW?" and, in 1993, a TV commercial introducing an "antitracking device for secret lovers everywhere."

People Who Dropped Their Surname

Angelina Jolie (born Angelina Jolie Voight)

Joe Louis (Joseph Louis Barrow)

Bela Lugosi (Bela Lugosi Blasko)

Sam Shepard (Samuel Shepard Rogers III)

David Blaine (David Blaine White)

Roger Vadim (Roger Vadim Plemmiankov)

Fiona Apple (Fiona Apple Maggart)

Ray Charles (Ray Charles Robinson)

Bonnie Bedelia (Bonnie Bedelia Culkin)

Eddie Albert (Edward Albert Heimberger)

Tom Cruise (Thomas Cruise Mapother IV)

Former Boxers

Kris Kristofferson, Chris Isaak, Terence Trent D'Arby, Berry Gordy, Billy Joel, Liam Neeson, Chuck Berry, Michael Flatley

A Guide to Golf

In the thirteenth century, the Dutch used to play a game known as *spel metten colve* ("game played with a club"). This became just *colve*, then *colf* and, eventually, "golf."

> **Robin Williams reckoned,** "Golf is a game where white men can dress up as black pimps and get away with it."

Winston Churchill described golf as "an ineffectual attempt to direct an uncontrollable sphere into an inaccessible hole with instruments ill-adapted to the purpose."

> **The first recorded hole-in-one** was scored by the great Tom Morris in 1868.

Bing Crosby died immediately after playing a round of golf.

> **When someone told Gary Player that he was "lucky,"** the great golfer replied, "That's funny, the more I practice, the luckier I get."

"Golf" spelled backward is "flog." Another thing to consider is that golf carts are better than caddies because golf carts can't count.

> **More people die playing golf** than any other sport—from heart attacks and lightning, et cetera.

Things Said by Groucho Marx

"Quote me as saying I was misquoted."

"I've had a perfectly wonderful evening. But this wasn't it."

"I was married by a judge. I should have asked for a jury."

"Now that I think of it, I wish I had been a hell-raiser when I was thirty years old. I tried it when I was fifty, but I always got sleepy."

"This would be a better world for children if parents had to eat the spinach."

"I've been around so long I can remember Doris Day before she was a virgin."

"From the moment I picked your book up until I laid it down, I was convulsed with laughter. Someday I intend reading it."

"A man's only as old as the woman he feels."

"Military justice is to justice what military music is to music."

"I must say that I find television very educational. The minute somebody turns it on, I go to the library and read a book."

"Women should be obscene and not heard."

"Time wounds all heels."

"Behind every successful man is a woman. Behind her is his wife."

"Outside of a dog, a book is man's best friend. Inside of a dog, it's too dark to read."

"Age is not a particularly interesting subject. Anyone can get old. All you have to do is live long enough."

"I sent the club a wire stating, 'Please accept my resignation. I don't care to belong to any club that will accept me as a member.'"

"It isn't necessary to have relatives in Kansas City in order to be unhappy."

"Money frees you from doing things you dislike. Since I dislike doing nearly everything, money is handy."

"Go, and never darken my towels again."

"Humor is reason gone mad."

"I didn't like the play, but then I saw it under adverse conditions—the curtain was up."

"I remember the first time I had sex—I kept the receipt."

"The secret of life is honesty and fair dealing. If you can fake that, you've got it made."

"When I was young, I was amazed at Plutarch's statement that the elder Cato began at the age of eighty to learn Greek. I am amazed no longer. Old age is

ready to undertake tasks that youth shirked because
they would take too long."

"I chased a girl for two years only to discover that her tastes
were exactly like mine: we were both crazy about girls."

"The husband who wants a happy marriage should learn to keep his mouth shut and his checkbook open."

"Here's to our wives and girl-friends . . . may they never meet."

"Paying alimony is like feeding hay to a dead horse."

"Well, art is art, isn't it? Still, on the other hand, water is
water! And east is east and west is west, and if you take
cranberries and stew them like applesauce, they taste
much more like prunes than rhubarb does. Now, you tell
me what you know."

"I'm going to Iowa for an award. Then I'm appearing at
Carnegie Hall—it's sold out. Then I'm sailing to
France to be honored by the French government. I'd
give it all up for one erection."

"Those are my principles. If you don't like them, I have
others."

Things Invented by Women

Fire escape, windshield wiper, laser printer, cotton gin, sewing machine, alphabet block, underwater telescope, cotton sewing thread (awarded the very first U.S. patent), brassiere, jockstrap, cordless phone, pulsar (discovered rather than invented), condensed milk, space suit, AIDS drugs AZT and protease inhibitors, TV dinner, Jell-O, Barbie doll, chocolate chip cookie, circular saw, dishwasher, disposable diaper, electric hot-water heater, ironing board, crash helmet, life raft, medical syringe, rolling pin, rotary engine, Scotchgard fabric protector

The Only People to Have Received Honorary U.S. Citizenship Granted by Act of Congress

Winston Churchill (1963), Raoul Wallenberg (1981), William and Hannah Penn (1984), Mother Teresa (1996)

The Simpsons

The characters of Homer, Marge, Lisa and Maggie were given the same first names as *Simpsons* creator Matt Groening's real-life father, mother and two sisters.

On *The Simpsons* **Monopoly board,** TIRE YARD is the cheapest property, while BURNS MANOR is the most expensive.

In an episode of *The Simpsons*, Sideshow Bob's criminal number is 24601—the same as Jean Valjean's prison number in *Les Misérables.*

"Appeared" on *The Simpsons*

Danny Devito (Herb Powell)

Jack Lemmon (Frank Ormand, the Pretzel Man)

Donald Sutherland (Hollis Hurlbut)

Joe Mantegna (Fat Tony)

Willem Dafoe (Commandant)

Tracey Ullman (Emily Winthrop)

Johnny Cash (Coyote)

Kirk Douglas (Chester J. Lampwick)

Rodney Dangerfield (Larry Burns)

Anne Bancroft (Dr. Zweig)

Penny Marshall (Ms. Botz)

Harvey Fierstein (Karl)

Glenn Close (Mother Simpson)

Gillian Anderson (Scully)

David Duchovny (Mulder)

Jackie Mason (Rabbi Krustofski)

Beverly D'Angelo (Lurleen Lumpkin)

Kelsey Grammer (Sideshow Bob)

Michelle Pfeiffer (Mindy Simmons)

Sam Neill (Molloy)

Kathleen Turner (Stacy Lovell)

Winona Ryder (Allison Taylor)

Meryl Streep (Jessica Lovejoy)

Patrick Stewart (Number One)

Susan Sarandon (The Ballet Teacher)

Mandy Patinkin (Hugh Parkfield)

Albert Brooks (Hank)

Jeff Goldblum (MacArthur Parker)

Dustin Hoffman (Mr. Bergstrom)

Cloris Leachman (Mrs. Glick)

Elizabeth Taylor (Baby Maggie)

John Waters (John)

James Earl Jones (The Narrator)

Ed Asner (Editor of the *Springfield Shopper*)

John Goodman (Meathook)

Henry Winkler (Ramrod)

Tim Robbins (Jim Hope)

Lisa Kudrow (Alex Whitney)

Robert Englund (Freddy Krueger)

Isabella Rossellini (Astrid Weller)

Michael McKean (Jerry Rude)

Martin Sheen (Sergeant Seymour Skinner)

Helen Hunt (Renée)

Rod Steiger (Captain Tenille)

Steve Martin (Ray Patterson)

Drew Barrymore (Sophie)

Patrick McGoohan (Prisoner #6)

Michael Keaton (Jack)

Pierce Brosnan (Computer)

Ben Stiller (Garth Motherloving)

Reese Witherspoon (Greta Wolfcastle)

Eric Idle (Desmond)

Professor Frink Senior (Jerry Lewis)

Played Themselves on
The Simpsons

Buzz Aldrin, Paul Anka, Tony Bennett, Ernest Borgnine, Mel Brooks, James Brown, Johnny Carson, David Crosby, Dennis Franz, Joe Frazier, George Hamilton, Hugh Hefner, Bob Hope, Magic Johnson, Tom Jones, Tom Kite, Linda McCartney, Paul McCartney, Bette Midler, Bob Newhart, Leonard Nimoy, Luke Perry, Linda Ronstadt, Mickey Rooney, Brooke Shields, Ringo Starr, Sting, Elizabeth Taylor, James Taylor, Adam West, Barry White, James Woods, Stephen Hawking, Britney Spears, Mel Gibson, Mark McGwire, Tom Arnold, Lucy Lawless, Dick Clark, Ron Howard, Penn and Teller, Butch Patrick, Gary Coleman, Bachman Turner Overdrive, Betty White, Ed McMahon, Regis Philbin, Kathie Lee Gifford, Jerry Springer, Alec Baldwin, Kim Basinger, the Moody Blues, Cyndi Lauper, Rupert Murdoch, Dolly Parton, Ed Begley Jr., Elton John, Joe Namath, Jay Leno, U2, Elvis Costello, Mick Jagger, Keith Richards, Lenny Kravitz, Tom Petty, Mark Hamill, Kid Rock, Willie Nelson, Pete Townshend, Roger Daltrey, Stephen King, Richard Gere, Little Richard, Tony Blair, J. K. Rowling, Ian McKellen

Flowers

The chrysanthemum is never grown in the Japanese city of Himeji because of a legend about a girl called O-Kiku ("Chrysanthemum Blossom") who drowned, leaving behind a troubled spirit that could be settled only if the people of Himeji didn't grow the flower of her name.

The tiger lily in Lewis Carroll's *Through the Looking Glass* claims that flowers talk "when there's anybody worth talking to," but that "in most gardens they make the beds too soft, so that the flowers are always asleep."

When a fan tried to present the great Italian conductor Arturo Toscanini with flowers at the end of a performance, he said, "They are for prima donnas or corpses: I am neither."

Dame *Iris* Murdoch on the subject of flowers: "People from a planet without flowers would think we must be mad with joy the whole time to have such things about us."

What William Wordsworth said about daffodils:

"*I wandered lonely as a cloud*
That floats on high o'er vales and hills.
When all at once I saw a crowd,
A host, of golden daffodils."

Wild Plant Names

Baldmoney, bastard balm, bloody cranes-bill, butcher's broom, creeping Jenny, devil's bit scabious, enchanter's nightshade, fairy foxglove, fat hen, fool's parsley, Good King Henry, hairy violet, hemlock water dropwort, hogweed, hound's tongue, Jack-by-the-hedge, Jacob's ladder, lady's bedstraw, lady's tresses, lamb's ear, leopard's bane, lords and ladies, love-in-a-mist, mind-your-own-business, purple loosestrife, red-hot Poker, scarlet pimpernel, shepherd's purse, Solomon's seal, stinking hellebore, traveler's joy, twiggy spurge, Venus's looking glass, viper's bugloss, wavy hair grass

People Who Had a Flower or Plant Named After Them

Madonna (gladiolus)

Dame Edna Everage (gladiolus)

Emma Bunton (bergamot)

Audrey Hepburn (fuchsia)

Elvis Presley (sempervivum)

Ricky Martin (orchid—*Renaglottis* Ricky Martin is yellow and crimson and produces lasting flowers all year)

Whoopi Goldberg (rose)

Vegetarians

Jude Law, Leonardo DiCaprio, Danny DeVito, Charlie Watts, Belinda Carlisle, Dustin Hoffman, Christie Brinkley, Billy Idol, Kim Basinger, Seal, Billy Connolly, Gwyneth Paltrow, Ted Danson, Daryl Hannah, Richard Gere, Julie Christie, Candice Bergen, Rosanna Arquette, Brooke Shields, Paul Newman, Peter Gabriel, Boy George, Martina Navratilova, Ian McKellen, LaToya Jackson, Prince, Ringo Starr, Terence Stamp, Michael Jackson, Whitney Houston, Michael Bolton, Morrissey, Chrissie Hynde, Lenny Kravitz, Ricki Lake, Vanessa Williams, Don McLean, Ozzy Osbourne, Stevie Nicks, Paul McCartney, Kate Bush, Elvis Costello, Bob Dylan, Yoko Ono, Jerry Seinfeld, Penelope Cruz, Tobey Maguire, Shania Twain (during her impoverished childhood, she made traps to catch rabbits for the family to eat), Willem Dafoe, Naomi Watts, Josh Hartnett, Angela Bassett, Anna Paquin, Forest Whitaker, Lauren Bush, Mena Suvari, Shannon Elizabeth, Natalie Portman, Alec Baldwin, Pamela Anderson, Nastassja Kinski, Ricky Martin

Lapsed Vegetarians

Liv Tyler, Paul Weller, Jeanette Winterson, Drew Barrymore

Pure Trivia, VI

An artist from Chicago named Dwight Kalb created a statue of Madonna made out of 180 pounds of ham.

About 10 million bacteria live in a gram of soil.

The record for finishing the Rubik's Cube is 16.5 seconds.

Nintendo was established in 1889 and started out making playing cards.

"Himalaya" means "home of snow."

The range of a medieval longbow was 220 yards.

The steepest street in the world is Baldwin Street in Dunedin, New Zealand, with an incline of 38 percent.

Watermelons, which are 92 percent water, originated from the Kalahari Desert in Africa.

Goat meat contains up to 45 percent less saturated fat than chicken meat.

The sound made by the Victoria Falls in Zimbabwe can be heard forty miles away.

Pumpkins were once recommended for removing freckles.

According to a rscheearch at Cmabgride Uinevrtisy, it deson't mtater waht oerdr the ltteres in a wrod are—so lnog as the frist and lsat ltteer are in the crorcet pclae. Tihs is bcuseae we dno't raed ervey lteter but the wrod as a wlohe.

Americans eat approximately 20 billion pickles every year.

In Belgium, there is a strawberry museum.

Sheep buried in snowdrifts can survive for up to two weeks.

Worldwide, grapes are grown more than any other fruit.

The mongoose was brought to Hawaii to kill rats, but the project failed because rats are nocturnal while the mongoose hunts during the day.

Rhode Island is the smallest U.S. state, but it has the longest official name: Rhode Island and Providence Plantations.

If you were locked in a completely sealed room, you'd die of carbon dioxide poisoning before you'd die of oxygen deprivation.

There are 556 officially recognized Native American tribes.

The last time American green cards were actually green was 1964.

Harvard uses "Yale" brand locks on its buildings.

The (American) football huddle originated in the nineteenth century at Gallaudet University, Washington D.C., when the deaf football team found that opposing teams were reading their signed messages and intercepting plays.

In the 1994 soccer World Cup the entire Bulgarian team had surnames ending with the letters *ov.*

Charles Lindbergh took just four sandwiches with him on his famous transatlantic flight.

Carnivorous animals will not eat another animal that has been hit by a lightning strike.

A mule is the offspring of a female horse and a male donkey, but the offspring of a male horse and a female donkey is called a hinny.

Isaac Newton was an ordained priest in the Church of England.

Dalmatian dogs are born pure white and only get their spots when they're a few days old.

"Heroin" is the brand name of morphine once marketed by Bayer.

The tango originated as a (practice) dance between two men.

Ben & Jerry's send their waste to local pig farmers to use as feed. Pigs love all the flavors except Mint Oreo.

Politics

"A government which robs Peter to pay Paul can always depend on the support of Paul." (George Bernard Shaw)

"Politics is the art of looking for trouble, finding it everywhere, diagnosing it incorrectly and applying the wrong remedy." (Groucho Marx)

"Politicians are the same all over. They promise to build a bridge even where there's no river." (Nikita Khrushchev)

"A politician is an ass upon which everyone has sat except a man." (e. e. cummings)

"Democracy must be something more than two wolves and a sheep voting on what to have for dinner." (James Bovard)

"Giving money and power to government is like giving whiskey and car keys to teenage boys." (P. J. O'Rourke)

"Just because you do not take an interest in politics doesn't mean politics won't take an interest in you." (Pericles in 430 B.C.)

"Suppose you were an idiot. And suppose you were a member of Congress. But I repeat myself." (Mark Twain)

"I believe that all government is evil, and that trying to improve it is largely a waste of time." (H. L. Mencken)

"The inherent vice of capitalism is the unequal sharing of the blessings. The inherent blessing of socialism is the equal sharing of misery." (Winston Churchill)

A Guide to Different Political Systems

Communism—You have two cows. The government takes both and gives you a little sour milk.

Fascism—You have two cows. The government takes both, hires you to take care of them, and sells you the milk.

Bureaucracy—You have two cows. To register them, you fill in twenty-three forms in triplicate and don't have time to milk them.

Socialism—You have two cows. The government takes one of them and gives it to your neighbor.

Feudalism—You have two cows. Your lord takes some of the milk.

Democracy—You have two cows. A vote is held, and the cows win.

Environmentalism—You have two cows. The government bans you from milking or killing them.

Libertarianism—Go away. What I do with my cows is none of your business.

Capitalism—You have two cows. You sell one and buy a bull.

N.B.: Surrealism—You have two porcupines. The government invites you to take cello lessons.

Things You Didn't Know About U.S. Presidents

Before winning the 1860 U.S. presidential election, Abraham Lincoln had lost eight elections for various offices.

Abraham Lincoln's mother died when the family dairy cow ate poisonous mushrooms and Mrs. Lincoln drank the milk.

Robert Todd Lincoln, son of Abraham Lincoln, was present at the assassinations of three U.S. presidents: Lincoln, Garfield and McKinley.

There are more handwritten letters in existence by George Washington (1789–97) than there are by John F. Kennedy (1961–63).

In 1849, David Atchison became president of the United States for just one day (most of which he spent sleeping).

John Quincy Adams (1825–29) owned a pet alligator, which he kept in the East Room of the White House. His wife, Louisa Adams, was the first (and only) foreign-born first lady of the United States; she was born in London.

Lyndon Johnson's (1963–68) family all had the initials LBJ: Lyndon Baines Johnson, Lady Bird Johnson, Linda Bird Johnson and Lucy Baines Johnson. His dog was called Little Beagle Johnson.

Theodore Roosevelt's (1901–12) wife and mother died on the same day.

On New Year's Day, 1907, Theodore Roosevelt shook hands with 8,150 people at the White House.

Since World War II, every U.S. president who has addressed the Canadian House of Commons in his first term of office has been reelected to a second term. Eisenhower, Nixon, Reagan and Clinton all did so, while Kennedy, Johnson, Ford, Carter and Bush Sr. didn't.

Every U.S. president with a beard has been Republican.

Franklin Pierce (1853–57) was the first president to have a Christmas tree in the White House.

Gerald Ford (1974–77) was the only president never to have been elected as either president or vice president.

N.B.: Daniel Webster, a nineteenth-century U.S. congressman, wanted to be president. He was offered the vice presidency by William Henry Harrison but turned it down. Then Harrison died in office. Again Webster was offered the vice presidency, by Zachary Taylor, but turned it down. Taylor, too, died in office, and Webster never did become president.

U.S. Presidents Who Won with Less Than Half the Popular Vote

1824—John Quincy Adams (Democratic-Republican: 30.5 percent) beat Andrew Jackson (Democratic-Republican: 43.1 percent), Henry Clay (Democratic-Republican: 13.2 percent) and William H. Crawford (Democratic-Republican: 13.1 percent)

1844—James K. Polk (Democrat: 49.58 percent) beat Henry Clay (Whig 48.12 percent) and James G. Birney (Liberty: 2.3 percent)

1848—Zachary Taylor (Whig: 47.33 percent) beat Lewis Cass (Democrat: 42.54 percent) and Martin Van Buren (Free Soil: 10.13 percent)

1856—James Buchanan (Democrat: 45.32 percent) beat John C. Frémont (Republican: 33.13 percent) and Millard Fillmore (American: 21.55 percent)

1860—Abraham Lincoln (Republican: 39.83 percent) beat Stephen A. Douglas (Democrat: 29.46 percent), John C. Breckinridge (Southern Democrat: 18.1 percent) and John Bell (Constitutional Union: 12.61 percent)

1876—Rutherford B. Hayes (Republican: 48.03 percent) beat Samuel J. Tilden (Democrat: 51.06 percent)

1880—James A. Garfield (Republican 48.3 percent) beat Winfield S. Hancock (Democrat: 48.28 percent) and James B. Weaver (Greenback-Labor: 3.32 percent)

1884—Grover Cleveland (Democrat: 48.52 percent) beat James G. Blaine (Republican: 48.27 percent), Benjamin F. Butler Greenback-Labor/Anti-Monopoly: 1.74 percent) and John P. St. John (Prohibition: 1.47 percent)

1888—Benjamin Harrison (Republican: 47.86 percent) beat Grover Cleveland (Democrat: 48.66 percent), Clinton B. Fisk (Prohibition: 2.2 percent) and Anson J. Streeter (Union Labor: 1.29 percent)

1892—Grover Cleveland (Democrat: 46.08 percent) beat Benjamin Harrison (Republican: 42.99 percent), James B. Weaver (People's: 8.5 percent) and John Bidwell (Prohibition: 2.25 percent)

1912—Woodrow Wilson (Democrat: 41.85 percent) beat Theodore Roosevelt (Progressive: 27.39 percent), William H. Taft (Republican: 23.19 percent), Eugene V. Debs (Socialist: 5.99 percent) and Eugene W. Chafin (Prohibition: 1.38 percent)

1916—Woodrow Wilson (Democrat: 49.33 percent) beat Charles E. Hughes (Republican: 46.2 percent), A. L. Benson (Socialist: 3.19 percent) and J. Frank Hanly (Prohibition: 1.19 percent)

1948—Harry S. Truman (Democrat: 49.56 percent) beat Thomas E. Dewey (Republican: 45.07 percent), Strom Thurmond (States' Rights Democrat: 2.41

percent) and Henry Wallace (Progressive: 2.37 percent)

1960—John F. Kennedy (Democratic: 49.94 percent) beat Richard M. Nixon (Republican: 49.77 percent)

1968—Richard M. Nixon (Republican: 43.43 percent) beat Hubert H. Humphrey (Democrat: 42.73 percent) and George C. Wallace (American Independent: 13.54 percent)

1992—Bill Clinton (Democrat: 43.02 percent) beat George Bush (Republican: 37.46 percent) and H. Ross Perot (Independent: 18.91 percent)

1996—Bill Clinton (Democrat: 49.15 percent) beat Robert Dole (Republican: 40.86 percent), H. Ross Perot (Independent: 8.48 percent), Ralph Nader (Green: 0.63 percent) and Harry Browne (Libertarian: 0.5 percent)

2000—George W. Bush (Republican: 47.87 percent) beat Al Gore (Democrat: 48.38 percent) and Ralph Nader (Green: 2.74 percent)

(N.B.: Where the percentages total less than 100 percent, it is because of unlisted minor-party candidates who polled fewer than 1 percent.)

The British House of Commons

MPs can wave their order papers and shout "hear, hear" to signal approval of a speech, but they're not allowed to clap.

Electronic voting equipment is not used: MPs must still walk through the "Aye" and "No" lobbies.

If an MP wants to empty the public galleries he has only to say, "I spy strangers."

MPs are not allowed to mention the House of Lords. They have to call the House of Lords "the other place."

There are yeomen dressed in Tudor uniform who ritually search the cellars of the House of Commons for gunpowder.

The Sergeant-at-Arms, whose office dates back to King Richard II, wears a cocked hat, a cutaway coat, knee breeches, a lace ruffle, black stockings and silver-buckled shoes.

MPs must not mention other MPs by name. Instead they must refer to them by their constituencies (e.g., "The member for . . .").

The Speaker of the House of Commons is obliged to show extreme reluctance on taking office.

Mayors

Clint Eastwood—Carmel, California

Sonny Bono—Palm Springs, California

Anthony Hopkins—Pacific Palisades (suburb of Los Angeles, California)

Ben & Jerry's Top Ten Flavors

Cherry Garcia Ice Cream

Chocolate Chip Cookie Dough Ice Cream

Chocolate Fudge Brownie Ice Cream

New York Super Fudge Chunk Ice Cream

Chunky Monkey Ice Cream

Half Baked Ice Cream

Phish Food Ice Cream

Cherry Garcia Frozen Yogurt

Peanut Butter Cup Ice Cream

Chocolate Fudge Brownie Frozen Yogurt

Charles Dickens

Dickens's father was a navy pay clerk who was laid off and ended up in debtors' prison. Young Charles worked in a blacking factory to help the family's finances.

Dickens used his father as the inspiration for Mr. Micawber, the ever-optimistic character from *David Copperfield*. W. C. Fields played the part of Micawber in the Hollywood film version and, when told that Dickens hadn't written anything about Micawber juggling, replied, "He probably forgot."

Later Dickens became a journalist—working first as a court reporter and eventually graduating to editor.

Dickens was prone to fainting fits. He gave dramatic readings of his books and sometimes worked himself up into such a state of excitement that he keeled over.

Dickens was an insomniac. He was also a little neurotic about his insomnia—always making sure that his bed pointed due north and that he was positioned in the absolute center of it.

In his letters to his wife, Kate, Dickens called her his "dearest mouse" and his "darling pig."

Dickens fell "deeply and intimately" in love with his wife's sister, Mary, when she came to live with them. Mary died at the age of seventeen, and Dickens wore her ring for the rest of his life. He asked to be buried next to her but was buried in Westminster Abbey instead.

After Mary, Dickens fell for another of his wife's sisters—Georgina—who came to live with them. When Dickens and his wife separated after twenty-two years of marriage (and ten children), Georgina stayed with him.

Write Poetry

Bob Hoskins, Ray Davies, David Carradine, Robert Downey Jr., Woody Harrelson, Traci Lords, Judd Nelson, Michael J. Pollard, Carl Reiner, Robbie Williams, Charisma Carpenter, Pamela Anderson, Denzel Washington, Brandy, Courtney Love and Russell Crowe (together), Christina Aguilera, Val Kilmer (for Michelle Pfeiffer), Kate Moss, Viggo Mortensen

Leap Years

February 29 occurs once every four years because, instead of precisely 365 days in a year, there are approximately 365¼. That is, it takes the earth 365¼ days to go around the sun and complete an astronomical year. The extra day every four years allows the man-made calendar to catch up with the astronomical calendar.

Leap years occur in any year that is divisible by 4, except those divisible by 100, though the 100 rule doesn't apply to those divisible by 400. So although 1900 was divisible by 4, it wasn't a leap year, but 2000 was. Thought: if there are 52 weeks in the year and 7 days in a week, why aren't there 364 days in the year?

Leap years are so called because, with 365-day years, a day of the month falling on Monday in one year will fall on a Tuesday in the next and on Wednesday in the third, but when the fourth year comes along with its extra day, it will "leap" over the Thursday to fall instead on the Friday.

On a Leap Year Day in 1956, a Mrs. Christine McDonnell of Church Street, Dublin, gave birth to a set of twins. On the next Leap Year Day, in 1960, she gave birth to another set of twins.

On Leap Year Day in 1984, Lisa Dluchik of Swindon, U.K., was born. Her mother, Suzanne, was also born on Leap Year Day (1956). The odds against a mother and a daughter both being born on February 29 have been calculated as 2 million to 1.

Things that have happened on Leap Year Day in history: In 1960, the Moroccan city of Agadir was devastated by an earthquake followed by a tidal wave that killed more than 12,000 people. In 1956, Pakistan became an Islamic republic. In 1960, Hugh Hefner opened his first Playboy Club (in Chicago)

Born on Leap Year Day

Gioacchino Rossini (1792)

Ranchhodji Desai (1896)

Jimmy Dorsey (1904)

Dinah Shore (1916)

Joss Ackland (1928)

Anthony Robbins (1960)

Hendrik Sundstrom (1964)

Pickup Lines

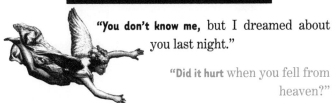

"You don't know me, but I dreamed about you last night."

"Did it hurt when you fell from heaven?"

"If I could rearrange the alphabet, I'd put U and I together."

"Can I buy you a drink, or do you just want the money?"

"Do you believe in love at first sight, or shall I walk past you again?"

"How do you like your eggs? Fertilized?"

"This body leaves in five minutes. Be on it."

"Your clothes would look great on my bedroom floor."

"Can I have your picture so I can show Santa what I want for Christmas?"

"I may not be the best-looking guy in the room, but I'm the only one talking to you."

"You're a thief—you've stolen my heart!"

"You remind me of someone I'd like to know."

"Can I borrow your cell phone? I told my parents I'd call them when I met the girl of my dreams."

"Is it me, or do you always look this good?"

"I need a map, because I'm lost in your eyes."

"The word 'beautiful' wouldn't be the same without U."

Migraine Cures

Pills are available without prescription: aspirin, paracetomol and ibuprofen—either in generic form or as branded drugs.

Regular exercise This will help *prevent* migraines. Also make sure blood pressure is under control, and don't smoke.

Diet Eat regular meals—every two hours if possible. Never miss breakfast. Eat a diet rich in carbohydrates. Avoid red wine, chocolate, cheese and citrus fruits.

Acupuncture In Denmark, doctors found that acupuncture was almost as effective as drugs against migraine, but without any of the side effects.

Regular sleep Too little or, interestingly, too much sleep can cause migraines. This is why a lot of people suffer from migraines on a Sunday when they've slept later than usual.

Mental well-being Hypertension, stress, suppressed anger, anxiety and depression are all causes/contributory factors of migraines. If your migraines are frequent, try to alleviate the states of mind that might be causing them.

Special rose-tinted eyeglasses, initially developed for children In tests, the average number of migraine attacks suffered by children ages 8 to 14 fell from 6.2 to 1.6 per month when they wore these glasses. According to the head of the retina department of the U.K.'s Birmingham's Eye Hospital, "The spectacles are just as effective in preventing migraine in grown-ups as they are in children."

Work Controversially, there are neurologists who believe that *not* giving in to a migraine, if possible, will see it off. A study of doctors who had worked through their migraines indicated that "work suppressed their migraine . . . although once they reached home they took to bed."

Botox injections People who've been to a botox clinic have found that their migraines have mysteriously disappeared. Now people have the treatment for this reason.

Unconsummated Marriages

Mary, Queen of Scots and Prince Francis of France

George Bernard Shaw and Charlotte Townsend

Burt Lancaster and June Ernst

Zsa Zsa Gabor and Burhan Belge

Zsa Zsa Gabor and Count Felipe de Alba

Prince Arthur (King Henry VIII's older brother) and Catherine of Aragon

Jean Harlow and Paul Bern

Rudolph Valentino and Jean Acker

Rudolph Valentino and Natasha Rambova

King Henry VIII and Anne of Cleves

Peter Tchaikovsky and Antonina Milyukova

Catherine and Peter the Great

André Gide and Madeleine Rondeaux

Fanny Brice and Frank White

Judy Garland and Mark Herron

Giuseppe Garibaldi and Giuseppina Raimondi

N.B.: It took Marie Antoinette and King Louis XVI *seven* years to consummate their marriage.

Married Their Childhood Sweetheart

Dick Cheney, Perry Como, Ray Winstone, Seve Ballesteros, Justine Henin-Hardenne, George Segal, Robert Smith, Ron Howard, Jon Bon Jovi, Tom Jones, Bono, Stephen King, Jeff Daniels, Al Gore, Carol Channing, Padraig Harrington

Married and Divorced Their Childhood Sweetheart

Harrison Ford, Sally Field, Michael Bolton, Sam Torrance, Gerhard Schröder, Sean Bean, Eminem, Richard Burton, Alan Cumming, Judy Collins

Whom They Chose as Their Best Man

GROOM	BEST MAN
Ronald Reagan	**William Holden**
Paul McCartney	Mike McGear (both times)
Jack Nicholson	**Harry Dean Stanton**
William Shatner	Leonard Nimoy
Vincente Minnelli	**Ira Gershwin**
Dougray Scott	Ewan McGregor
Patrick Stewart	**Brent Spiner**
David Gest	Michael Jackson
Larry Fortensky	**Michael Jackson**
David Beckham	Gary Neville
Rowan Atkinson	**Stephen Fry**
Peter Sellers	David Lodge
Mick Jagger	**Lord Patrick Lichfield**
Jake La Motta	Sugar Ray Robinson
Christopher Hitchens	**Martin Amis**
Martin Amis	Christopher Hitchens
Josef Goebbels	**Adolf Hitler**

Engagements That Didn't Lead to Marriage

Michelle Pfeiffer and Fisher Stevens

Ronan Keating and Vernie Bennett

Van Morrison and Michelle Rocca

Olivia Newton-John and Bruce Welch

Shannen Doherty and Dean Factor

Axl Rose and Stephanie Seymour

Adam Sandler and Margaret Ruden

Laura Dern and Billy Bob Thornton

Eriq LaSalle and Angela Johnson

Robbie Williams and Nicole Appleton

Heath Ledger and Naomi Watts

Ben Affleck and Gwyneth Paltrow

Pamela Anderson and Kid Rock

Lenny Kravitz and Adriana Lima

Alan Cumming and Saffron Burrows

Fred Couples and Tawnya Dodd

Carole Landis and Busby Berkeley

Emma Samms and Marvin Hamlisch

Princess Stephanie of Monaco and Jean-Yves LeFur

Charlie Sheen and Kelly Preston (later married to John Travolta)

Victoria Adams (now Beckham) and Mark Wood

Sharon Stone and Michael Benasra

Yasmine Bleeth and Ricky Paull Goldin

Virgins on Their Wedding Day

Shirley Temple, Lisa Kudrow, Donny Osmond, Elizabeth Taylor, Priscilla Presley, Ava Gardner, Loretta Lynn, Raquel Welch, Catherine the Great, Mark Twain, Vivien Leigh, Gloria Swanson, Mrs. Patrick Campbell, Colette, Hedda Hopper, Mary Martin, Paul Muni

Marriages That Didn't Last

Zsa Zsa Gabor and Count Felipe de Alba (one day)

Britney Spears and Jason Alexander (one day)

Ethel Merman and Ernest Borgnine (four days)

Dennis Rodman and Carmen Electra (nine days)

Dennis Rodman and Annie Banks (twelve days)

Burt Lancaster and June Ernst (one month)

Henry Fonda and Margaret Sullavan (two months)

Aaliyah and R. Kelly (three months—annulled because she was just fifteen)

Janet Jackson and James DeBarge (four months)

Natasha Henstridge and Damian Chapa (five months)

Drew Barrymore and Tom Green (five months)

Elton John and Renate Blauel (a few months)

Don Johnson and Melanie Griffith (the first marriage—a few months)

Arthur C. Clarke and Marilyn Mayfield (six months)

Christie Brinkley and Ricky Taubman (seven months)

Axl Rose and Erin Everly (seven months)

Dennis Wilson and Karen Lamm (seven months the first time; two weeks the second time)

Jean Harlow and Hal Rosson (eight months)

Kelsey and Leanne Grammer (eight months)

Dodi Fayed and Suzanne Gregard (eight months)

Emma Samms and Bansi Nagji (eight months)

Judy Garland and David Rose (eight months)

Jennifer Lopez and Cris Judd (eight months)

Marilyn Monroe and Joe DiMaggio (nine months)

Suzanne Pleshette and Troy Donahue (nine months)

Jim Carrey and Lauren Holly (ten months)

Ellen Terry and George Watts (ten months)

Alyssa Milano and Cinjun Tate (ten months and nineteen days)

Paul Simon and Carrie Fisher (eleven months)

Helen Hunt and Hank Azaria (eleven months)

Sarah Bernhardt and Aristides Damala (less than a year)

Whoopi Goldberg and Dave Claessen (less than a year)

Sheena and Sandi Easton (nine months)

Sheena Easton and Timothy Delarm (less than a year)

Sheena Easton and Robert Light (one year)

Sheena Easton and John Minoli (seventeen months)

Named as Co-Respondents in Divorce Cases

Warren Beatty (in the divorce of Peter Hall and Leslie Caron)

Mick Jagger (Marianne Faithfull and John Dunbar)

George Weidenfeld (Cyril Connolly and Barbara Skelton)

Cyril Connolly (George Weidenfeld and Barbara Skelton—this was the order in which this remarkable true-life soap occurred)

Olivia Newton-John (Bruce and Ann Welch)

W. Somerset Maugham (Henry and Syrie Wellcome)

Sexual Offers That Were Turned Down

Marianne Faithfull turned down Bob Dylan and Jimi Hendrix.

Marlon Brando turned down Tallulah Bankhead and Anna Magnani.

Olivia de Havilland turned down Errol Flynn and Leslie Howard.

Marlene Dietrich turned down Ernest Hemingway and Adolf Hitler (after approaches to her were made by Goebbels and von Ribbentrop on his behalf).

Britt Ekland turned down Ron Ely.

Ava Gardner turned down Howard Hughes.

Mary Pickford turned down Clark Gable.

Greta Garbo turned
down Aristotle
Onassis.

Evelyn Keyes turned down
Harry Cohn.

Katharine Hepburn
turned down
Douglas Fairbanks Jr. and John Barrymore.

Jean Simmons turned down John F. Kennedy and Howard Hughes.

Veronica Lake turned down Errol Flynn.

Laurence Olivier turned down Merle Oberon.

Lana Turner turned down Mickey Rooney.

Joan Collins turned down Daryl F. Zanuck and Richard Burton.

Tallulah Bankhead turned down John Barrymore.

Jean Harlow turned down Louis B. Mayer.

Clara Bow turned down Al Jolson.

Zizi Jeanmaire turned down Howard Hughes (this was after he'd brought over the entire ballet company for a film—purely to seduce her).

Gina Lollobrigida turned down Howard Hughes.

Vaslav Nijinsky turned down Isadora Duncan.

Gertrude Stein turned down Ernest Hemingway.

Ava Gardner turned down George C. Scott.

Jaclyn Smith turned down Warren Beatty.

Bette Davis turned down Joan Crawford (according to Hollywood legend—although their lifelong enmity is equally likely to be due to the fact that Davis had an affair with Franchot Tone while he was married to Crawford).

Marilyn Monroe turned down Joan Crawford.

Anthony Perkins turned down Ingrid Bergman.

Jacqueline Susann turned down Coco Chanel.

Rita Hayworth turned down Harry Cohn.

Bette Davis turned down Miriam Hopkins.

Merle Oberon turned down Stewart Granger.

Janet Leigh turned down Howard Hughes.

Tyrone Power turned down Norma Shearer.

Grace Kelly turned down Bing Crosby.

Paul McCartney turned down Little Richard.

Mrs. Patrick Campbell turned down George Bernard Shaw.

John Wayne turned down Marlene Dietrich.

Celebrities Who Lost Their Virginity with Another Celebrity

Amanda Donohoe with Adam Ant

Juliette Lewis with Brad Pitt

Mary Astor with John Barrymore Sr.

Debbie Reynolds with Eddie Fisher

Ava Gardner with Mickey Rooney

Nastassja Kinski with Roman Polanski

Malcolm Maclaren with Vivienne Westwood

Brigitte Bardot with Roger Vadim

Cecil Beaton with Adele Astaire

Elliott Gould with Barbra Streisand

Brooke Shields with Dean Cain

Priscilla Beaulieu with Elvis Presley

Gloria Swanson with Wallace Beery

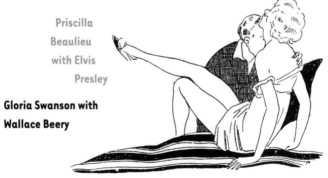

Members of the Mile-High Club

Bill Clinton

Mel B

Julia Roberts and Jason Patric

Tori Spelling

Dennis Rodman (on the Concorde)

Pamela Anderson Lee and Tommy Lee (in a toilet on a flight from L.A. to New York. She said, "It was fantastic. When we came out, everyone clapped and cheered.")

John Travolta and Kelly Preston (on the private jet back to America from France where they were married)

John Cusack

The Maharaja of Baroda

Leonardo DiCaprio (hired an executive jet, served a girl strawberries and ice cream and then made love looking at the stars)

Kelsey Grammer (with his then-wife)

Kylie Minogue (with Michael Hutchence—in first class, just a few seats away from the Australian PM)

Carmen Electra ("The craziest place I made love was in an airplane, in the bathroom. I thought it was hot, I loved it.")

307

Richard Branson ("before Virgin Atlantic")

Jane Fonda and Ted Turner (on his private jet in 1991)

Björn Borg (on a flight from Copenhagen to New York)

Men Who Lost Their Virginity with a Prostitute

Henry Fonda, David Niven (with a London girl nicknamed Nessie), Uri Geller (a Greek-Cypriot girl named Lola), Anton Chekhov, Chris De Burgh (with a French girl), Napoleon Bonaparte, James Joyce, John F. Kennedy (the girl charged three dollars), Benito Mussolini, Stendhal, Leo Tolstoy, H. G. Wells, Groucho Marx, Mike Tyson, Richard Branson, Ilie Nastase, Colin Farrell (taken there by his father)

N.B.: According to Ian Fleming, James Bond lost his virginity in Paris at the age of 16 with a prostitute named Martha Debrant.

Age at Which They Lost Their Virginity

AGE 13

Curt Smith, Peter Andre, Justin Hayward (with a girl of 20)

AGE 14

David Chokachi, David Niven, James Joyce

AGE 15

John Barrymore (with his stepmother), Shelley Winters, Peter O'Toole, Art Buchwald, Burt Reynolds, Tina Turner, Jack London (with a girl who "came with" a boat he bought), Uri Geller, Sting, Lisa Marie Presley (with a 24-year-old drug dealer), Sally Field

AGE 16

Benito Mussolini, Grigory Rasputin, Leo Tolstoy, Jean Harlow, Carmen Electra ("It was in Cincinnati in the backseat of a car. It was not very glamorous, and I don't remember it being such a great experience"), Mel C, Richard Harris, Teri Hatcher, Raquel Welch, Shirley MacLaine, Ursula Andress, Robert Burns, Shelley Duvall, Groucho Marx, Barbara Hutton, Jayne Mansfield, Mike Tyson

AGE 17

Ginger Rogers, Alexandre Dumas Sr, Steven Spielberg, Cyndi Lauper, Erica Jong, Carrie Fisher, Dyan Cannon, Mary Astor, Alicia Silverstone, Donna D'Errico (in a car), Dr. Ruth Westheimer

AGE 18

Victoria Principal, Vivien Leigh, Susan Hayward

AGE 19

Lillian Hellman, Alison Steadman

AGE 22

Libby Holman

AGE 23

Debbie Reynolds, Catherine the Great, Hugh Hefner

AGE 39

Johann von Goethe

Things Said About Sex

"I believe that sex is a beautiful thing between two people. Between *five*, it's fantastic. . . ." (Woody Allen)

"When women go wrong, men go right after them." (Mae West)

"My father told me all about the birds and the bees. The liar—I went steady with a wood-pecker till I was twenty-one." (Bob Hope)

"Sex is one of the nine reasons for reincarnation—the other eight are unimportant." (Henry Miller)

"It sounds strange for me to be saying this, but I've come around to the idea that sex really is for procreation." (Eric Clapton)

"**Being a sex symbol** is a heavy load to carry—especially when one is tired, hurt and bewildered." (Marilyn Monroe)

"**It's strange to become a sex symbol at forty.** And even to be described as a kind of Warren Beatty. The truth is that, until I met my wife at thirty-five, I only had two girl-friends." (Colin Firth)

"**I come from a strict Catholic upbringing**, and sex was a taboo subject. That makes you crave sex ten times more for the rest of your life." (Salma Hayek)

"**Sex is about as important as a cheese sandwich.** But a cheese sandwich, if you ain't got one to put in your belly, is extremely important." (Ian Dury)

"**The only unnatural sexual behavior** is none at all." (Sigmund Freud)

"**All this fuss about sleeping together;** for physical pleasure, I'd sooner go to my dentist any day." (Evelyn Waugh)

"**It's been so long since I made love** I can't remember who gets tied up." (Joan Rivers)

"**Sex appeal is fifty percent** what you've got and fifty percent what people think you've got." (Sophia Loren)

"**It has to be admitted that we English** have sex on the brain—which is a very unsatisfactory place to have it." (Malcolm Muggeridge)

"**Sex**—the poor man's polo." (Clifford Odets)

"It [sex] ruins friendships between men and women."
(Julia Roberts)

"I'm never through with a girl until I've had her three ways."
(John F. Kennedy)

"If I took all my clothes off, I wouldn't be sexy anymore.
I'd just be naked. Sex appeal is about keeping
something back." (Jennifer Lopez)

"I believe that sex is the most beautiful, natural and wholesome
thing that money can buy." (Steve Martin)

"Conventional sexual intercourse is like squirting jam
into a doughnut." (Germaine Greer)

"The greatest pleasure that one person can offer another is
carnal pleasure." (Coco Chanel)

"I've never considered myself addicted to anything,
but if I was, sex was it." (Clint
Eastwood)

"What comes first in a relationship is
lust, then more lust." (Jacqueline
Bisset)

"Sex is a bad thing because
it rumples the clothes."
(Jacqueline Kennedy
Onassis)

"A man with an erection is in
no need of advice."
(Samuel Pepys)

"**The number of available orgasms** is fixed at birth and can be expended. A young man should make love very seldom or he will have nothing left for middle age." (Ernest Hemingway)

"**Sex has never interested me much.** I don't understand how people can waste so much time over sex. Sex is for kids, for movies—it's a great bore." (Alfred Hitchcock)

"**Sex is as important** as food and drink." (Britt Ekland)

"**Some things are better than sex** and some things are worse, but there's nothing exactly like it." (W. C. Fields)

"**If you were married to Marilyn Monroe**—you'd cheat with some ugly girl." (George Burns)

"**The minute you start fiddling around outside** the idea of monogamy, nothing satisfies anymore." (Richard Burton)

"**Accursed from their birth they be** / Who seek to find monogamy. / Pursuing it from bed to bed— / I think they would be better dead." (Dorothy Parker)

"**You know, of course, that the Tasmanians,** who never committed adultery, are now extinct." (W. Somerset Maugham)

Pure Trivia, VII

Velcro was invented by a Swiss man who noticed the way burrs attached themselves to clothing.

Physicist Murray Gell-Mann picked the name "quarks" from a line in James Joyce's *Ulysses:* "Three quarks for Muster Mark!"

When a film is in production, the last shot of the day is known as "the Martini shot."

Native speakers of Japanese learn Spanish much more easily than they learn English.

The distress term "Mayday" comes from the French term *m'aidez,* meaning "help me."

In Disney's *Fantasia,* the Sorcerer's name is Yensid, which is Disney backward.

A metal coat hanger is 44 inches long when straightened.

The most common name in Italy is Mario Rossi.

Roosters can't crow if their necks aren't fully extended.

Shirley Temple always had 56 curls in her hair.

The three largest landowners in England are Queen Elizabeth II, the Church of England and Trinity College, Cambridge.

Most American car horns beep in the key of F.

Goldfish can suffer motion sickness.

Dirty Harry's badge number was 2211.

The United States has never lost a war in which mules were used.

All gondolas in Venice have to be painted black unless they belong to a high official.

Rhinos are thought to have inspired the myth of the unicorn.

The sport with the highest ratio of officials to participants is tennis. A singles match should have 13: 10 line umpires, 1 net official, 1 foot-fault official and 1 chair umpire.

The shortest intercontinental commercial flight is from Gibraltar (Europe) to Tangier (Africa.). The distance is 34 miles, and the flight takes 20 minutes.

The quartz crystal in a wristwatch vibrates 32,768 times a second.

The United States has more bagpipe bands than Scotland.

There's no sand in sandpaper.

Mark Wahlberg has a third nipple (airbrushed out of the Calvin Klein underwear ad).

Elvis Presley never gave an encore.

Gone with the Wind was set in the U.S. Civil War but didn't feature a single battle scene.

Flamingo tongues were a delicacy in ancient Rome.

Kellogg's Tony the Tiger turns 50 in 2005.

The Jolly Green Giant turns 77 in 2005.

The YKK on a zipper stands for Yoshida Kogyo Kabushi-bibaisha, the world's largest zipper manufacturer.

Before 1800, there was no such thing as separate shoes for left and right feet.

A Guide to French Fries

The fry was first made in France—hence the name "french fries."

In Britain, the first mention of fries is to be found in an 1854 recipe book, *Shilling Cookery,* in which chef Alexis Soyer referred to a recipe with "thin cut potatoes cooked in oil."

In 1857, Charles Dickens referred to plates of "potato sticks cooked in oil."

Gram for gram, fries contain a quarter of the fat of doughnuts.

Fries are the biggest-selling frozen vegetable in the world.

Only the British sprinkle their chips with vinegar. The French usually have a pinch of salt, the Belgians use mayonnaise, while the Americans use ketchup.

In 1996, the Irish introduced edible bags for fries to cut down on litter. According to someone who ate one, the bags "taste a bit like mashed potato."

Vogue **magazine** ran into trouble when it published a recipe that recommended using horse lard to cook tastier french fries.

In the nineteenth century, British fish-and-chip fryers were social outcasts because of the strong odor of frying that remained on their clothes.

Fries are a good source of vitamin C and complex carbohydrates in the form of starch. They also provide protein, fiber, iron and other vitamins.

Every year British fish-and-chip shops chop up 500,000 tons of potatoes for chips—that's one-twelfth of all the potatoes eaten in Britain.

The Germans have invented a revolutionary oven that produces a greaseless chip.

The actress Cameron Diaz says she has a "love affair with french fries," which plays havoc with her skin. "I've always been a salty, greasy kind of girl," she declares.

Nick Faldo shocked the American golfing establishment when he ordered fries for the 1997 Masters Dinner. As defending champion, it was up to him to choose the menu for the Past Champions Dinner in the Augusta National clubhouse. After his two previous victories, he chose steak and kidney pie and shepherd's pie, but in 1997 he selected British fish, chips and, of course, mushy peas.

In *Pulp Fiction*, John Travolta, as Vincent Vega, the heroin-addled hit man, tells Samuel L. Jackson, "Did you know McDonald's serves french fries with mayonnaise in Amsterdam?"

Height Index

4 foot 11: Charlene Tilton, Lil' Kim

5 foot: Dawn French, Geraldine Chaplin, Jada Pinkett Smith

5 foot 1: Kylie Minogue, Danny DeVito, Sheena Easton, Carrie Fisher, Debbie Reynolds, Stevie Nicks, Lucy Liu

5 foot 2: Holly Hunter, Sally Field, Joan Rivers, Linda Ronstadt, Sissy Spacek, Gloria Estefan, Joan Collins, Judi Dench, Emma Bunton, Geri Halliwell, Reese Witherspoon

5 foot 3: Mickey Rooney, Sarah Michelle Gellar, Christina Aguilera, Helena Bonham Carter, Kathy Bates

5 foot 4: Madonna, Michael J. Fox, Roman Polanski, Drew Barrymore, Britney Spears, Queen Elizabeth II, Tina Turner, Scarlett Johansson

5 foot 5: Belinda Carlisle, Mel B, Jennifer Aniston, Joe Pesci

5 foot 6: Princess Anne, Calista Flockhart, Victoria Beckham, Elijah Wood

5 foot 7: Mick Jagger, Laetitia Casta, Tom Cruise, Kate Winslet, Catherine Zeta-Jones, Mark Wahlberg, Keira Knightley

5 foot 8: Phil Collins, Rita Coolidge, Lauren Hutton, Billy Joel, Ringo Starr, Robin Williams, Robert Redford, Mel Gibson, Ali Landry, Elizabeth Hurley, Tobey Maguire, Mackenzie Crook, Ricky Gervais

5 foot 9: Lauren Bacall, Prince Charles, Shannon Elizabeth, Cameron Diaz

5 foot 10: Naomi Campbell, Lily Tomlin, Nicole Kidman, Natasha Henstridge, Gwyneth Paltrow, Minnie Driver

5 foot 11: George Michael, Bea Arthur, Vanessa Redgrave, Brooke Shields, Sigourney Weaver, Claudia Schiffer, Jerry Hall, Lucy Lawless, Sophie Dahl

6 foot: Eva Herzigova, Brad Pitt, Macy Gray, Tony Blair, Leonardo DiCaprio, Matthew Perry, Allison Janney

6 foot 1: Pete Sampras, Venus Williams, Pierce Brosnan, Freddie Prinze Jr., Chris Isaak, Enrique Iglesias

6 foot 2: Lindsay Davenport, Tiger Woods, Timothy Dalton

6 foot 3: Clint Eastwood, Muhammad Ali, Jon Voight, Al Gore, Brendan Fraser

6 foot 4: Chevy Chase, Louis Gossett Jr., Ralph Nader, Tom Selleck, Ben Affleck, Goran Visnijc, Benicio Del Toro, Heath Ledger, Rupert Everett, John Kerry

6 foot 5: Mick Fleetwood, Tim Robbins, Howard Stern

6 foot 6: Dolph Lundgren, Tommy Tune, Hulk Hogan

6 foot 7: John Cleese

6 foot 9: Michael Crichton

7 foot 2: Richard Kiel

Brains

The brain is the second-heaviest organ in the human body (after the liver and ahead of the lungs and the heart).

A brain weighs around three pounds. All but ten ounces is water.

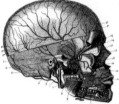

The brain uses more than 25 percent of the oxygen required by the human body.

The brain uses less power than a hundred-watt bulb.

Is eating fish good for the brain? Up to a point. The brain needs decosahexaenoic acid to develop, and this is found in oily fish.

Albert Einstein's brain was preserved after his death. So was Lenin's.

Vincent van Gogh's brain was destroyed by the mercury he took to counteract syphilis.

The Buffalo Theory

A herd of buffalo moves only as fast as the slowest buffalo. So when the herd is hunted, it is the weakest and slowest ones at the back that get killed first. This example of natural selection is beneficial for the herd, because the regular culling of the weakest animals improves the overall and average health and speed of the whole group. Similarly, the human brain can work only at the speed of its slowest cells. Now, too much alcohol kills brain cells—but, importantly, the weakest and slowest cells first. Consequently, regular beer consumption, by eliminating them, is making your brain work faster and better.

So the moral of this theory is, drink more beer.

Unintentionally Funny (Genuine) Newspaper Headlines

HIGH SCHOOL DROPOUTS CUT IN HALF

COMPLAINTS ABOUT REFEREES GROWING UGLY

ASBESTOS SUIT PRESSED

PHYSICIST RECOMMENDS BIGGER BALLS TO SLOW
DOWN MALE TENNIS PLAYERS

NEW STUDY OF OBESITY LOOKS FOR LARGER TEST GROUP

PUPILS TRAIN AS COUNSELORS TO HELP UPSET
CLASSMATES

TWO CONVICTS EVADE NOOSE: JURY HUNG

PANDA MATING FAILS—VETERINARIAN TAKES OVER

ORGAN FESTIVAL ENDS IN A SMASHING CLIMAX

DEALERS WILL HEAR CAR TALK AT NOON

TWO SISTERS REUNITE AFTER EIGHTEEN YEARS AT CHECK-
OUT COUNTER

POLICE DISCOVER CRACK IN AUSTRALIA

WAR DIMS HOPE FOR PEACE

BOY WANTS TO MOUNT AUTOGRAPHED GUITAR

BODY FOUND ON BOAT SEIZED BY BAILIFFS AND DUE TO BE
AUCTIONED

MILK DRINKERS ARE TURNING TO POWDER

TYPHOON RIPS THROUGH CEMETERY; HUNDREDS DEAD

BABIES USED TO SNEAK DRUGS INTO PRISON

ARAFAT SWEARS IN CABINET

BANGKOK LAUNCHES ANTI-BUTT CAMPAIGN

NEW AUTOS TO HIT 5 MILLION

MARCH PLANNED FOR NEXT AUGUST

NEW HOUSING FOR ELDERLY NOT YET DEAD

TUNA BITING OFF WASHINGTON COAST

JUDGE ACTS TO REOPEN THEATER

WOMAN ATTACKED BY TRAIN STATION

CHOPPER SEARCH FOR MAN IN UNDERPANTS

BRITON GORED BY BULL IN INTENSIVE CARE

BULGE IN TROUSERS WAS ECSTASY

CARIBBEAN ISLANDS DRIFT TO LEFT

SOMETHING WENT WRONG IN JET CRASH, EXPERT SAYS

GOLFERS WARNED NOT TO LICK BALLS

DRUGS FINE FOR BUSINESSMAN

COPS QUIZ VICTIM IN FATAL SHOOTING

SEX SCANDAL VICAR SEEKS NEW POSITION

CIRCUMCISION NOW SEEN AS POINTLESS

DOWN UNDER LOVE FOR PRINCESS ANNE'S DAUGHTER

BLIND BISHOP APPOINTED TO SEE

EU MUST UNITE ON DRUGS

GIANT TEA BAGS PROTEST

POLICE CHIEF'S PLEDGE TO MURDER WITNESSES

MOST SURGEONS FACE CUTS

12 ON THEIR WAY TO CRUISE AMONG DEAD IN PLANE CRASH

STIFF OPPOSITION EXPECTED TO CASKETLESS
FUNERAL PLAN

INCLUDE YOUR CHILDREN WHEN BAKING COOKIES

DAD WANTS BABY LEFT IN AIRPLANE

MALE NATURIST MEMBERS RISE

CUTS COULD HURT ANIMALS

CHEF THROWS HIS HEART INTO HELPING FEED NEEDY

PUBLIC SWINGS IN FAVOR OF THE PRINCE

HALF MILLION ITALIAN WOMEN SEEN ON PILL

IDAHO GROUP ORGANIZES TO HELP SERVICE WIDOWS

L.A. VOTERS APPROVE URBAN RENEWAL BY LANDSLIDE

LESOTHO WOMEN MAKE GREAT CARPETS

MAN WITH ONE ARM AND LEG CHEATS ON OTHER HALF

MEN RECOMMEND MORE CLUBS FOR WIVES

GUNMAN SHOT BY 999 COPS

PROSTITUTES TO HOLD OPEN DAY

SUBSTITUTE TEACHERS SEEKING RESPECT

NIGHT SCHOOL TO HEAR PEST TALK

HOME SECRETARY TO ACT ON VIDEO NASTIES

DIET OF PREMATURE BABIES "AFFECTS IQ"

SEX UP AND DOWN AFTER SEPTEMBER 11

LARGEST AMOUNT OF CANNABIS EVER SEIZED IN JOINT OPERATION

STRAW'S PLEDGE TO RAPE VICTIMS

MAD COW TALKS

The Senility Prayer

God, grant me the senility to forget the people I never liked anyway, the good fortune to run into the ones that I do and the eyesight to tell the difference.

Suicide

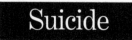

Three times as many men commit suicide as women. But women attempt suicide two to three times more often than men.

The season for suicides is the spring; the winter months have the lowest number of suicides.

In 1926, a Budapest waiter committed suicide. He left his suicide note in the form of a crossword, and the police had to get help from the public to solve it.

Vincent van Gogh committed suicide while painting *Wheat Field with Crows.*

Committed Suicide

Kurt Cobain, Michael Hutchence, Gig Young, Richard Manuel, Ian Curtis, Jerzy Kosinski, Terry Kath, Ron "Pigpen" McKernan, Donny Hathaway, Cleopatra, Ernest Hemingway, Margot Hemingway, Marc Antony, Del Shannon, Brian Epstein, John Kennedy Toole, Joseph Goebbels, Nick Drake, Phil Ochs, Yukio Mishima, George Sanders, Hannibal, Freddie Prinze, Primo Levi, Adolf Hitler, Nero, Kid McCoy, Pontius Pilate, Capucine, Carole Landis, Charles Boyer, Dorothy Dandridge, Hervé Villechaize, Faron Young, Pete Duel, the Singing Nun, George Reeves, Margaret Sullavan, Jean Seberg, Thelma Todd, Lupe Velez, Spalding Gray, Hunter S. Thompson

People Whose Father Committed Suicide

Ernest Hemingway, Tara Fitzgerald, Hal Ashby, Phil Spector (on his tombstone were the words "To know him was to love him"), Ted Turner, Betty Hutton, Slobodan Milosevic, Ben Hogan, Martina Navratilova, Alger Hiss, Jean Cocteau

People Whose Mother Committed Suicide

Alan Ladd, Sid Vicious, Jane Fonda, Mike Oldfield, Slobodan Milosevic, René Magritte, Truman Capote, Mikhail Baryshnikov, Richard Todd, Spalding Gray, Jean-Bedel Bokassa, Amos Oz, Kurt Vonnegut, Peter Fonda

People Whose Son Committed Suicide

Gregory Peck, Theodore Roosevelt, Paul Newman, Bing Crosby (two sons), Ian Fleming, Dan Dailey, Mary Tyler Moore, Bobby Womack, Thomas Mann, Charles Boyer, Richard Todd, Eugene O'Neill (two sons), Art Linkletter, Carroll O'Connor, Walter Winchell, Judy Collins

People Whose Daughter Committed Suicide

Margaret Sullavan, Karl Marx, Robert Frost, James Arness, Marlon Brando, John Barrymore, Timothy Leary

Men Whose Wife Committed Suicide

Adolf Hitler (with him), Timothy Leary, Jackson Browne, Arthur Koestler (with him), Joseph Goebbels (with him), Joseph Stalin, Henry Fonda

Women Whose Husband Committed Suicide

Courtney Love, Katharine Graham, Joan Rivers

Survived Suicide Attempts

Drew Barrymore, Elton John, Marianne Faithfull, Frank Sinatra, Tuesday Weld, Billy Joel, Brenda Fricker, Sinéad O'Connor, Vanilla Ice, Mickey Rooney, Yannick Noah, Pamela Anderson, Mel B, Halle Berry, Jack Osbourne, Judy Collins

Enough to End It All?

In 1927, Edwin Wakeman of Manchester committed suicide, leaving this note: "I married a widow with a grown daughter. My father fell in love with my stepdaughter and married her—thus becoming my son-in-law. My stepdaughter became my stepmother because she was my father's wife. My wife gave birth to a son, who was, of course, my father's brother-in-law, and also my uncle, for he was the brother of my stepmother. My father's wife became the mother of a son, who was, of course, my brother, and also my grandchild, for he was the son of my stepdaughter. Accordingly, my wife was my grandmother, because she was my stepmother's mother. I was my wife's husband and grandchild at the same time. And, as the husband of a person's grandmother is his grandfather, I am my own grandfather."

Died Onstage (Literally)

Tommy Cooper (comedian/magician)

Sid James (actor)

Leonard Rossiter (actor)

Marie Lloyd (singer)

Simon Barere (pianist)

Les Harvey (Stone the Crows musician—electrocuted by touching a live microphone with wet feet in 1972)

Richard Versalle (opera singer—after singing the line "Too bad you can only live so long")

Linda Wright (nightclub singer)

Leonard Warren (opera singer)

Died Virgins

Immanuel Kant, Nikolai Gogol, Queen Elizabeth I, Isaac Newton, Anton Bruckner, Hans Christian Andersen

Died Intestate

Jayne Mansfield, George Gershwin, Karl Marx, Rita Hayworth, Howard Hughes, Abraham Lincoln, Pablo Picasso, Duke Ellington, Lenny Bruce, Paolo Gucci, Sylvia Plath, Keith Moon, Robert Johnson

Believe in Reincarnation

Jesper Parnevik, Joan Collins, k. d. lang, Keanu Reeves, Conchita Martinez, Tori Amos, Shirley MacLaine, Gillian Anderson, Sarah Jessica Parker, William H. Macy

Famous Men's Last Words

"I'm still alive." (Caligula, A.D. 41)

"Tomorrow, I shall no longer be here." (Nostradamus—possibly the only prophecy he got right, 1566)

"Friends, applaud, the comedy is over." (Ludwig van Beethoven, 1827)

"Such is life." (Ned Kelly, 1880)

"Who is it?" (Billy the Kid before being shot by Sheriff Pat Garrett, 1881)

"Go on, get out! Last words are for fools who haven't said enough." (Karl Marx, 1883)

"So little done, so much to do." (Cecil Rhodes, 1902)

"Four o'clock. How strange. So that is the time. Strange. Enough." (Henry Morton Stanley, 1904)

"It is never too late for a glass of champagne." (Anton Chekhov, 1904)

"Don't let it end like this. Tell them I said something."
(Pancho Villa, 1923)

"I'm tired of fighting. I guess this is going to get me." (Harry Houdini, 1926)

"If this is dying, I don't think much of it." (Lytton Strachey, 1932)

"Never felt better." (Douglas Fairbanks Sr., 1939)

"But, but, Mister Colonel . . ." (Benito Mussolini, 1945)

"Go away. I'm all right." (H. G. Wells, 1946)

"Born in a hotel room and—Goddamn it—died in a hotel room." (Eugene O'Neill, 1953)

"Dying is easy. Comedy is difficult." (Edmund Gwenn, 1959)

"Oh, God, here I go." (Max Baer, 1959)

"Dying is a very dull affair. My advice to you is to have nothing whatever to do with it." (W. Somerset Maugham, 1965)

"It hurts." (Charles de Gaulle, 1970)

"Drink to me." (Picasso, 1973)

"Okay, I won't." (Elvis Presley, after his girlfriend told him not to fall asleep in the bathroom, 1977)

"That was a great game of golf, fellas." (Bing Crosby, 1977)

N.B.: When Albert Einstein died in 1955, his final words died with him—the nurse at his side didn't understand German.

Died Before the Age of 40

King Louis XVII of France, 10

King Edward V, 12

St. Agnes, 13

St. Pancras, 14

Anne Frank, 15

King Edward VI, 16

Ritchie Valens, 17

Tutankhamen, 18

Joan of Arc, 19

Catherine Howard, 20

Dorothy Stratten, 20

Eddie Cochran, 21

Stu Sutcliffe, 21

Sid Vicious, 21

Aaliyah, 22

Billy the Kid, 22

Pocahontas, 22

Buddy Holly, 22

Freddie Prinze, 22

Bonnie Parker, 23

River Phoenix, 23

Duane Allman, 24

Tammi Terrell, 24

Lee Harvey Oswald, 24

James Dean, 24

Frankie Lymon, 25

Clyde Barrow, 25

Françoise Dorléac, 25

John Keats, 25

Baron Manfred von Richthofen, 25

Gram Parsons, 26

Otis Redding, 26

Sharon Tate, 26

Nick Drake, 26

Kurt Cobain, 27

Jimi Hendrix, 27

Robert Johnson, 27

Brian Jones, 27

Janis Joplin, 27

Ron "Pigpen" McKernan, 27

Jim Morrison, 27

Bix Beiderbecke, 28

Caligula, 28

Brandon Lee, 28

J. P. Richardson (aka "The Big Bopper"), 28

Karen Silkwood, 28

Marc Bolan, 29

Fletcher Christian, 29

Ronnie Van Zant, 29

Hank Williams, 29

Anne Brontë, 29

Percy Bysshe Shelley, 29

Jean Vigo, 29

Emily Brontë, 30

Jim Croce, 30

Jeff Buckley, 30

Andreas Baader, 30

Steve Biko, 30

Brandon DeWilde, 30

Andy Gibb, 30

Lisa "Left Eye" Lopes, 30

335

Nero, 30

Keith Moon, 31

John Bonham, 31

Sandy Denny, 31

Pete Duel, 31

Karen Quinlan, 31

Minnie Riperton, 31

John Kennedy Toole, 31

Rudolph Valentino, 31

Patsy Cline, 31

Florence Ballard, 32

John Dillinger, 32

Queen Mary II, 32

King Richard III, 32

Jane Seymour, 32

Robert Walker, 32

Bruce Lee, 32

Karen Carpenter, 32

Bill Hicks, 32

Carole Lombard, 33

Dick Turpin, 33

Alexander the Great, 33

John Belushi, 33

Eva Braun, 33

Sam Cooke, 33

Mama Cass Elliot, 33

Sanjay Gandhi, 33

Donny Hathaway, 33

Eva Perón, 33

King Richard II, 33

Yuri Gagarin, 34

Ayrton Senna, 34

Jayne Mansfield, 35

Charlie Parker, 35

Stevie Ray Vaughan, 35

Wolfgang Mozart, 35

Jesse James, 35

King Henry V, 35

Phil Ochs, 35

Peter Revson, 35

Marilyn Monroe, 36

Robespierre, 36

George Custer, 36

Rainer Werner Fassbinder, 36

Bob Marley, 36

Mike Bloomfield, 36

Princess Diana, 36

Bob "The Bear" Hite, 36

Marie Antoinette, 37

Bobby Darin, 37

Lou Gehrig, 37

Michael Hutchence, 37

Sal Mineo, 37

Christina Onassis, 37

Irving Thalberg, 37

Vincent van Gogh, 37

Georges Bizet, 37

Alexander Pushkin, 37

Robert Burns, 37

Charlotte Brontë, 38

Felix Mendelssohn, 38

Harry Chapin, 38

Stephen Foster, 38

George Gershwin, 38

Amelia Earhart, 38

Florence Griffith Joyner, 38

John Kennedy Jr., 38

Mario Lanza, 38

Federico García Lorca, 38

Che Guevara, 39

Frédéric Chopin, 39

Dylan Thomas, 39

Dr. Martin Luther King Jr., 39

Blaise Pascal, 39

Dennis Wilson, 39

Pier Angeli, 39

Neil Bogart, 39

Tim Hardin, 39

Wild Bill Hickok, 39

Jim Reeves, 39

Fats Waller, 39

Dinah Washington, 39

Malcolm X, 39

Emiliano Zapata, 39

Grace Metalious, 39

John Garfield, 39

Died in a Plane Crash

Roald Amundsen (1928)

Will Rogers (1935)

Carole Lombard (1942)

Leslie Howard (1943)

Charles Paddock (1943)

Antoine de Saint-Exupéry (1944)

Glenn Miller (1944)

Mike Todd (1958)

Duncan Edwards (1958)

Buddy Holly (1959)

J. P. Richardson ("The Big Bopper," 1959)

Ritchie Valens (1959)

Dag Hammarskjöld (1961)

Patsy Cline (1963)

Jim Reeves (1964)

Herbert Marshall (1966)

Otis Redding (1967)

Yuri Gagarin (1968)

Rocky Marciano (1969)

died in a plane crash

Audie Murphy (1971)

Prince William of Gloucester (1972)

Jim Croce (1973)

Graham Hill (1975)

Ronnie Van Zant (1977)

Steve Gaines (1977)

Cassie Gaines (1977)

Sanjay Gandhi (1980)

Ricky Nelson (1985)

Larry Shue (1985)

Muhammad Zia ul-Haq (1988)

Stevie Ray Vaughan (1990)

John Tower (1991)

Bill Graham (1991)

Ron Brown (1996)

John Denver (1997)

Payne Stewart (1999)

John F. Kennedy Jr. (1999)

Aaliyah (2001)

Died in a Road Accident

T. E. Lawrence [of Arabia] (1935)

Tom Mix (1940)

George S. Patton (1945)

Margaret Mitchell (1949)

James Dean (1955)

Jackson Pollock (1956)

Prince Aly Khan (1960)

Eddie Cochran (1960)

Albert Camus (1960)

Ernie Kovacs (1962)

Jayne Mansfield (1967)

Françoise Dorléac (1967)

Duane Allman (1971)

Brandon De Wilde (1972)

Marc Bolan (1977)

Harry Chapin (1981)

Grace Kelly (1982)

Falco (1988)

Diana, Princess of Wales (1997)

Dodi Fayed (1997)

Ian Bannen (1999)

Desmond Llewelyn (1999)

Lisa "Left Eye" Lopes (2002)

Helmut Newton (2004)

The Last Line of Every Shakespeare Play

All's Well That Ends Well: "Your gentle hands lend us, and take our hearts." (King)

Antony and Cleopatra: "Come, Dolabella, see / High order in this great solemnity." (Octavius Caesar)

As You Like It: "If I were a woman, I would kiss as many of you as had beards that pleased me, complexions that liked me and breaths that I defied not: and, I am sure, as many as have good beards, or good faces, or sweet breaths, will, for my kind offer, when I make curtsy, bid me farewell." (Rosalind)

The Comedy of Errors: "Nay, then, thus: / We came into the world like brother and brother; / And now let's go hand in hand, not one before another." (Dromio of Ephesus)

Coriolanus: "Though in this city he / Hath widow'd and unchilded many a one, / Which to this hour bewail the injury, / Yet he shall have a noble memory.—Assist." (Aufidius)

Cymbeline: "Never was a war did cease, / Ere bloody hands were wash'd, with such a peace." (Cymbeline)

Hamlet: "Take up the bodies: such a sight as this / Becomes the field, but here shows much amiss. / Go, bid the soldiers shoot." (Fortinbras)

Henry IV, Part One: "Rebellion in this land shall lose his sway, / Meeting the check of such another day: / And since this business so fair is done, / Let us not leave till all our own be won." (Henry IV)

Henry IV, Part Two: "I will lay odds that, ere this year expire, / We bear our civil swords and native fire / As far as France: I heard a bird so sing, / Whose music, to my thinking, pleas'd the king. / Come, will you hence?" (Lancaster—followed by an epilogue)

Henry V: "Then shall I swear to Kate, and you to me; / And may our oaths well kept and prosperous be!" (Henry V—followed by a chorus)

Henry VI, Part One: "Margaret shall now be queen, and rule the king; / But I will rule both her, the king, and realm." (Suffolk)

Henry VI, Part Two: "Sound drums and trumpets, and to London all: / And more such days as these to us befall!" (Warwick)

Henry VI, Part Three: "Sound drums and trumpets! farewell sour annoy! / For here, I hope, begins our lasting joy." (Edward IV)

Henry VIII: "This day, no man think / Has business at his house; for all shall stay: / This little one shall make it holiday." (Henry VIII—followed by an epilogue)

Julius Caesar: "So call the field to rest; and let's away, / To part the glories of this happy day." (Octavius)

King John: "Nought shall make us rue, / If England to itself do rest but true." (Bastard)

King Lear: "The weight of this sad time we must obey; / Speak what we feel, not what we ought to say. / The oldest hath borne most: we that are young / Shall never see so much, nor live so long." (Albany)

Love's Labor's Lost: "The words of Mercury are harsh after the songs of Apollo. You that way: we this way." (Armado)

Macbeth: "Of this dead butcher and his fiend-like queen, / Who, as 'tis thought, by self and violent hands / Took off her life; this, and what needful else / That calls upon us, by the grace of Grace, / We will perform in measure, time, and place: / So, thanks to all at once, and to each one, / Whom we invite to see us crown'd at Scone." (Malcolm)

Measure for Measure: "So, bring us to our palace; where we'll show / What's yet behind that's meet you all should know." (Duke Vicentio)

The Merry Wives of Windsor: "Let it be so. Sir John, / To Master Brook you yet shall hold your word / For he, tonight, shall lie with Mistress Ford." (Ford)

The Merchant of Venice: "Well, while I live, I'll fear no other thing / So sore as keeping safe Nerissa's ring." (Gratiano)

A Midsummer Night's Dream: "So, good night unto you all. / Give me your hands, if we be friends, / And Robin shall restore amends." (Puck)

Much Ado About Nothing: "Think not on him till tomorrow: / I'll devise thee brave punishments for him. / Strike up, pipers." (Benedick)

Othello: "To you, lord governor, / Remains the censure of this hellish villain; / The time, the place, the torture: O, enforce it! / Myself will straight aboard; and to the state / This heavy act with heavy heart relate." (Lodovico)

Pericles: "So, on your patience evermore attending, / New joy wait on you! Here our play has ending." (Gower)

Richard II: "Lords, I protest, my soul is full of woe, / That blood should sprinkle me to make me grow: / Come, mourn with me for that I do lament, / And put on sullen black incontinent: / I'll make a voyage to the Holy Land, / To wash this blood off from my guilty hand: / March sadly after; grace my mournings here; / In weeping after this untimely bier." (Henry Bolingbroke)

Richard III: "Now civil wounds are stopp'd, peace lives again: / That she may long live here, God say amen!" (Richmond)

Romeo and Juliet: "A glooming peace this morning with it brings; / The sun, for sorrow, will not show his head: / Go hence, to have more talk of these sad things; / Some shall be pardon'd, and some punished: / For never was a story of more woe / Than this of Juliet and her Romeo." (Prince)

The Taming of the Shrew: "'Tis a wonder, by your leave, she will be tamed so." (Lucentio)

The Tempest: "Now I want / Spirits to enforce, art to enchant, / And my ending is despair, / Unless I be relieved by prayer, / Which pierces so, that it assaults / Mercy itself, and frees all faults. / As you from crimes would pardon'd be, / Let your indulgence set me free." (Prospero)

Timon of Athens: "Bring me into your city, / And I will use the olive with my sword, / Make war breed peace; make peace stint war; make each / Prescribe to other, as each other's leech. / Let our drums strike." (Alcibiades)

Titus Andronicus: "See justice done on Aaron, that damn'd Moor, / By whom our heavy haps had their beginning: / Then, afterwards, to order well the state, / That like events may ne'er it ruinate." (Lucius)

Troilus and Cressida: "Brethren and sisters of the old-door trade, / Some two months hence my will shall here be made: / It should be now, but that my fear is this, / Some galled goose of

Winchester would hiss: / Till then I'll sweat, and seek about for eases; / And at that time, bequeath you my diseases." (Pandarus)

Twelfth Night: "Cesario, come: / For so you shall be while you are a man; / But, when in other habits you are seen, / Orsino's mistress, and his fancy's queen." (Duke—followed by Clown's song)

Two Gentlemen of Verona: "Come, Proteus; 'tis your penance but to hear / The story of your loves discovered: / That done, our day of marriage shall be yours; / One feast, one house, one mutual happiness." (Valentine)

The Winter's Tale: "Good Paulina, / Lead us from hence, where we may leisurely / Each one demand, and answer to his part / Perform'd in this wide gap of time, since first / We were dissever'd: hastily lead away!" (Leontes)

Finally . . .

"All I've ever wanted was an honest week's pay for an honest day's work." (Steve Martin)

"Early to rise and early to bed, makes a male healthy, wealthy and dead." (James Thurber)

"I like long walks, especially when they are taken by people who annoy me." (Fred Allen)

"**I think a man can have two,** maybe three affairs, while he is married, but three is maximum. After that, you're cheating." (Yves Montand)

"**You can kill,** you can maim people, but to be boring is truly a sin. And God will punish you for that." (Burt Reynolds)

"**Gluttony** is not a secret vice." (Orson Welles)

"**Wickedness** is a myth invented by good people to account for the curious attractiveness of others." (Oscar Wilde)

"**Tip big and tip quietly.** Fold the bills three times into small squares and pass them in a handshake." (Frank Sinatra)

"**Remember that as a teenager** you are in the last stage of your life when you will be happy to hear that the phone is for you." (Fran Lebowitz)

"**To his dog, every man is Napoleon,** hence the constant popularity of dogs." (Aldous Huxley)

"**Life is a tragedy** when seen in close-up but a comedy in long-shot." (Charlie Chaplin)

"**Happiness in life is good health** and a bad memory." (Ingrid Bergman)

"**I do not believe** that friends are necessarily the people you like best; they are merely the people who got there first." (Peter Ustinov)

"**I did not become a vegetarian** for my health. I did it for the health of the chickens." (Isaac Bashevis Singer)

"At fifty everyone has the face he deserves." (George Orwell)

"My best feature's my smile. And smiles—pray heaven—don't get fat." (Jack Nicholson)

"There are only two things a child will share willingly—communicable diseases and his mother's age." (Benjamin Spock)

"You never really know a man until you have divorced him." (Zsa Zsa Gabor)

"The worst part of having success is to try finding someone who is happy for you." (Bette Midler)

"Whenever a friend succeeds, a little something in me dies." (Gore Vidal)

"Punctuality is the virtue of the bored." (Evelyn Waugh)

"That is the essence of science: ask an impertinent question, and you are on the way to a pertinent answer." (Jacob Bronowski)

"When you sit with a nice girl for two hours, you think it's only a minute. But when you sit on a hot stove for a minute, you think it's two hours. That's relativity." (Albert Einstein)

"I can take any amount of criticism, so long as it is unqualified praise." (Noël Coward)

AUTHOR'S NOTE

I had so much fun compiling *That Book*—and the reaction to it was so gratifyingly (and surprisingly) generous—that I couldn't resist putting together this imaginatively entitled sequel.

As with the first book, most of it has been acquired "organically" over the past twenty years (yup, that's the sort of man I am). However, I am obliged to acknowledge material culled from the Internet—especially in the sections insects etc.; the human condition; fish, etc.; geography; birds, etc.; history; animals, etc.; and science. Apart from the indispensable Google, I used LexisNexis, the best and the most user-friendly search tool I've ever come across.

Meanwhile, I am still on the lookout for fascinating trivia and ideas that I might be able to use in a third book (inevitably entitled *The Other Book*). So if you have anything you think might be of interest—or even if you simply want to get in touch to point out all my mistakes—then please write to me at: thatbook@mail.com.

ACKNOWLEDGMENTS

This Book required ingenuity, cleverness and talent. Fortunately, I had the help of a group of people who possess such qualities by the bucketload. Step forward and take a bow (in alphabetical order): Hugh Adams, Luigi Bonomi, Penny Chorlton, Patrick Janson-Smith, Mari Roberts (even if she did talk me out of including the fascinating fact that the average person has fewer than two arms), David Roth-Ey and Doug Young.

In addition, I'd also like to thank the following people for their help, contributions and/or support (moral or otherwise): Jeremy Beadle, Marcus Berkmann, Jeremy Clarkson, Chris Ewins, Jonathan Fingerhut, Jenny Garrison, Richard Littlejohn, Tricia Martin, Emanuel Mond, William Mulcahy, Rex Newman, Jeanette Perez, Nicholas Ridge, Maureen Sugden, Charlie Symons, Jack Symons, Roy Wells, Katrina Whone, Rob Woolley and Stewart Wright.

If I've missed anyone, then please know that—as with any mistakes in the book—it's entirely down to my own stupidity.

LIST OF LISTS